"...a remarkable road map to guide families experiencing the trauma of divorce. It also provides a well marked path for those professionals who teach and care for children of divorce in the school system...the stop signs, the obstacles, the hurdles and warning signs are conspicuously evident along the way. And for each known problem, situation, Dr. Lapin offers a negative and positive solution...her own personal experience and professional skills make this book a necessary assist in addressing the impact created by divorce on families and society."

—Myra F. Levick, PhD, ATR-BC,
Author of *See What I'm Saying: What Children Tell Us Through Their Art*

"...an invaluable resource for parents, teachers, school administrators, parent counselors and attorneys representing children of divorce...covers all the specifics providing divorced parents with much needed advice on the details of co-parenting for school related issues."

—Elizabeth Thayer, Ph.D., Co-Author of
The Co-Parents Survival Guide: Letting Go of Conflict After a Difficult Divorce

"This bo͏   ͏se in fostering
positive   owards maxi-
mizing   with valuable
informat

    Nati͏   County, FL

"Dr. La   ficant issues
raised b   Her answers
to paren   obstacles of
divorce   !"

                                                  ordan, R.N.
                                                  ng Director

"..well w   parents. Dr.
Lapin en   ve them."

                                                  nan, Ph.D.,
                                                  g Program
                                              ...ᴄᴏᴜnty School Board

"...should be mandatory reading for all divorced parents...as well as school personnel who wish to help them. Dr. Lapin anticipates all the potential challenges affecting children of divorce and offers concise, caring and practical steps to ensure their emotional well-being."

—Helene Sorcic, School Social Worker
Broward County Schools, FL

"This is a must read for divorced parents with school age children. The book offers useful information to encourage both parents to be actively involved in their child's education. As an educator and a divorced parent of four, I found wonderful suggestions and solutions to daily issues that are encountered by divorced parents raising children together."

—Michelle Nevis
Special Ed Teacher, Woodstock High School

"A resource to help parents...Dr. Lapin has written the definitive guide to dealing with how custody affects school issues with a down-to-earth, practical approach to each and every area that divorced parents deal with in their children's schools. I would definitely recommend this book for my parents and have it in my library as a handy reference. Dr. Lapin has done a phenomenal job in the execution of this book."

—Theresa K. Sullivan, M.S., NBCT
Guidance Counselor, Broward County School Board, FL

"...it's about time someone wrote a 'how-to' for divorced parents...judges should have a stack to hand out upon divorcing the parents...reminding them that they have not divorced their children. I thank you for the parents who will read and follow the advice written...it sure will make our job easier."

—Sherri Holzman, Principal
Randazzo School, Broward County, FL

"...an exceptional guide for both parents and teachers...the format of the book is very 'user friendly' and it covers all the issues that parents must deal with while their child is in school. This book would be an excellent resource, which could be given to parents at conferences."

—Phyllis Bloom
High School Teacher, Maryland

School Days
&
THE DIVORCE MAZE

A COMPLETE GUIDE FOR JOINT CUSTODY PARENTS IN MANAGING YOUR CHILD'S SUCCESSFUL SCHOOL CAREER

Dr. Renae Lapin
Licensed Marriage & Family Therapist

Frederick Fell Publishers, Inc.
2131 Hollywood Blvd.,Suite 305
Hollywood, FL 33020
fellpub@aol.com
www.FellPub.com

Frederick Fell Publishers, Inc.
2131 Hollywood Blvd.,Suite 305
Hollywood, FL 33020
fellpub@aol.com
www.FellPub.com

Published by Frederick Fell Publishers, Inc.,
2131 Hollywood Blvd. Suite 305 Hollywood, Florida 33020

This publication is designed to provide accurate and authoritative information in regard to the subject matter covered. This book is not intended to replace the advice and guidance of a trained physician nor is it intended to encourage self-treatment of illness or medical disease. Although the case histories presented are true, all names of patients have been changed.

Library of Congress Cataloging-in Publication Data

Dr. Renae Lapin, LMFT 1955-
School Days and the Divorce Maze: A Complete Guide for Joint Custody Parents in Managing Your Child's Successful School Career
    p. cm.
ISBN 0-88391-162-0 (trade pbk.: alk paper)
1. Renae Lapin, 1955- 2. Family & Relationships: Divorce & Separation
LC5159 .L37 2007
371.19/2 22

                              2007032859
10 9 8 7 6 5 4 3 2 1

Dedication

To: The hundreds of children and families with whom I have been honored to work with throughout my twenty-eight year career as a Family Therapist; and to my own family of which I am lucky to be a part of.

Table of Contents

Preface

I wrote this book for use by divorced parents who share joint custody of their children. There is much advice published regarding the topic of divorce, parenting and education. Most contain little or no specific detailed advice as to how to manage the day to day school issues which become cumbersome for joint custody families. My work as a Family Therapist in a school setting often focused on these specific school issues. I noticed that when handled well by both parents, children flourished, exhibited a healthy self esteem, pride in their school and an interest in their education. Unfortunately, these school issues often became the battle ground or lightening rod for the conflict between the divorced couple. When that occurred, I witnessed children who were depressed, anxious and often completely devastated by a school experience.

As my career progressed, I too, became a joint custody divorced parent and struggled with the same difficult issues as my clients. I learned that schools are not equipped to respond to the needs of joint custody families and inadvertently place barriers for these children to develop a sense of comfort with their school.

All of the stories contained in this book are based upon true experiences of the children and families I have been honored to work with, as well as my personal experiences as a joint custody divorced parent. Names and identifying information have been changed to protect the confidentiality of the families I have worked with.

Introduction

***Why a complete guide especially for school issues is needed for joint
custody parents:***
 The legal spirit of joint custody addresses the concept that both parents
have equal rights, privileges and responsibilities regarding the important
aspects of their children's growth to adulthood. Financial responsibilities
and visitation schedules are spelled out clearly in your divorce decree. No
guidance as to how to handle specific school issues is given. As a divorced
parent, your perceptions and priorities may have become distorted as a
result of your feelings towards your ex-spouse. Although you truly have
your child's best interests at heart, your feelings towards the divorce and
your ex sometimes block you from using your common sense. This is
normal. Generally, you will do your best to promote your child's successful school career if you know exactly what to do. This book will give you
specific, clear steps on how to manage every big and small issue which
arises with your child's school career. The issues addressed in this book
will provide you with creative ideas in helping to teach your child responsibility and supporting a healthy self esteem. Most importantly, the ideas
in these chapters will alert you to potential negative experiences which
could cause trauma for your child. The examples presented are based upon
actual experiences of children from divorced homes. These children want
to alert you of potential conflicts which can be avoided with education,
common sense and putting your child's feelings and needs first. Often the
big issues are disguised as little issues – don't make the mistake of over-
looking them!

Message to primary residential custodial Parents
 The primary residential parent, or the parent with whom the child
lives with most of the time, has specific responsibilities toward their

child and their child's other parent regarding school issues. This is in the best interest of your child and critical to their successful school career, self esteem and future happiness. Each chapter of this book addresses your responsibility in managing every school issue with your ex, throughout your child's educational career. Situations that actually happened to children from divorced parents just like you help illustrate creative solutions to some of the same problems you experience. There are many examples of things you can do which require a little imagination and a little effort. This is a sacred privilege for you to undertake, honoring the great love you have for your child. You can make it happen!

Message to second custodial Parents

As a joint custodial parent who does not have his/her child living with them most of the time, you have specific rights, responsibilities and privileges regarding your child's schooling. Each one of these is detailed in the following chapters. You have a wonderful opportunity to influence your child's success in school, as well as his/her self esteem and happiness for the future. Many creative ideas are offered throughout these chapters for you to take an important role in influencing your child's educational career over the years. Small amounts of time and effort can result in lasting positive benefits for your child and your relationship with your child. Learn how to avoid having your child suffer from painful traumatic experiences. Real examples are provided with actual experiences of children from divorced homes. Take the time to develop special school memories for you and your child. You will not regret it!

Message to school age Children

Your success in school and happiness are very important to your parents. They can help you do your best every day. You need to share all of your school papers and feelings about school with your parents so they can do their best to help you to be successful. Divorced parents are just as concerned about their children's school success as married parents. This book gives you and your parents great ideas as to how to make it easier for your parents to help you in school! These ideas are explained with examples from other children, like yourself, who live with divorced parents. They may not feel exactly the same way you do in every situation, but you will probably find some experiences you can relate to. Tell your parents – they really do want to know how you feel! Really!!

Message to School Administrators

Divorced parents with joint custody are more and more common is schools today. You are in a unique position to set the tone of how your school manages these situations for the best interest of your students. This chapter offers specific suggestions for setting the tone in your school as well as specific policies and procedures in accommodating the unique needs of your students with divorced parents. School administrators just like you have grappled with these sticky situations. Your staff finds these issues difficult, frustrating and confusing. They rely on your leadership and clear policies as to how to best negotiate these conflicts. This responsibility is a privilege with a high rate of successful outcomes as measured by the success and happiness of the students who attend your school. Your students, parents and staff will appreciate your efforts. Take the time to try some of these ideas and be a pioneer in your district!

1. Recognize that there are many children in your school who have divorced joint custodial parents and spend part of their school week with both parents. This presents unique problems to these students. Some of these problems can be easily resolved, while others cannot be. Your recognition and sensitivity to the needs of these children, their families, and your teachers is the key.

2. Provide easy access to duplicate copies of all report cards, progress reports and notices home such as school field trips, school newsletter, school picture day, school calendar, open house day, etc. Explore the possibility of providing a duplicate set of textbooks to children living with two different parents during the school week.

3. Provide your teachers with direction and support as to how to manage highly conflictual joint custody parents when conducting

teacher conferences and other school events. This is extremely stressful to your teachers and they need your support and direction at these times. Support can be in the form of arranging a discussion with a plan before and after such a conference; or offering to sit in on the conference; or assign the school Guidance Counselor to sit in on the conference.

4. Provide your school Registrar and front office staff with a set of very clear directions as to how to manage requests from joint custodial parents. An understanding of the law, the school board policy and training in diffusing disruptive parents can be provided. They are your front line and often the initial contact for these families. The interaction with these key staff positions can set the stage for future interaction with these families.

5. Provide an opportunity for your school Guidance Counselor to be trained in leading small groups for children from divorced homes. Positive experiences have been reported by children who have attended such support groups at school, often leading to increased sense of self esteem and academic success.

6. Avoid setting a tone of judgment towards families with configurations other than the traditional family. You will be alienating the majority of your student population as well as many of your staff.

Message to Teachers

Many of your students are from divorced homes with joint custody being the norm, some living with alternating parents during the school week. All teachers need some help in knowing how to manage these complicated, sometimes volatile situations. You can increase the chances of your students' success in your classroom with some simple strategies that will be well worth your time. You can also help avoid the painful moments these children suffer in school which have the potential to lead to emotional trauma. You have a unique opportunity to make the difference! The following are some ideas of how you can help. Take the time to speak with your school Guidance Counselor and

Administrator at the beginning of the school year to try to set these ideas in motion:

1. Find out from your students at the beginning of the year who they live with and on which days. Some children have complicated visitation arrangements which would benefit you to be aware of in promoting their success in your classroom.

2. Let these children know that they are not alone, but that there have been others, or that there are currently others in your classroom with a similar situation and that you will do your best to accommodate to their unique living situation.

3. Provide children with two families a duplicate copy of all notices sent home, including school wide events and newsletters as well as report cards, progress reports and classroom events. Explore the option of two sets of textbooks for these children.

4. Have the student's parents let you know how they wish to handle communication from the school between both joint custody parents. Some sets of parents communicate very well with each other and will let you know that it is only necessary to provide information to one parent and it will automatically be passed on to the other parent. Other parents might not feel comfortable sitting in the same room with each other and school conferences may be needed to be conducted separately. Consult your administrator for direction in these highly conflictual joint custody arrangements.

5. Consider extending a personal invitation to the school to a joint custody parent who may be new to monitoring his or her child's academic progress and may feel uncomfortable doing so initially. It will promote your student's success in your classroom and overall academic growth if you go the extra mile in providing suggestions for specific academic activities and books to reinforce material taught in the classroom. Joint Custody parents are juggling a lot in their lives and will welcome specific creative

suggestions that can be worked into their schedule – this is your expertise!

6. Recognize that your student may be adjusting to a new living arrangement and may need help in developing a study routine and organization schedule for school.

7. Seek assistance from your administration and Guidance staff in identifying ways to promote a positive sense of self esteem and avoid unnecessary trauma for these children.

Part I

Academic
Issues

Chapter One

School Supplies: Tsunamis or Solutions

Which parent is responsible for purchasing school supplies for the year?

The primary custodial parent generally is responsible for purchasing the school supplies for the school year, however this should not be assumed by both parties. It might be more appropriate for the second custodial parent to purchase the school supplies, or for both parties to share the cost. This discussion should take place before the school year begins, between the adults only, making sure that the child(ren) do not overhear any disagreements about this issue. Sometimes the school will provide a list of supplies before the summer vacation, allowing parents plenty of time to stock up.

Who is responsible for replenishing these supplies throughout the school year?

The supplies are generally replenished by the primary residential parent unless discussed and prearranged by both parents.

Which school supplies should the secondary custodial parent keep at their home?

If the child is doing any schoolwork, homework, studying or projects at the second residential parent's home, a set of school supplies will be needed, depending upon the grade level. Consult your child's teacher for specifics, however, it would be good to have pens, pencils, paper, index cards, paper clips, highlighters, tape, glue, stapler, three ring hole puncher, colored pencils, ruler, calculator, dictionary, thesaurus, computer and supervised use of internet.

Who is responsible for last minute supplies for a project?

Children are notorious for requesting last minute supplies for a school project. The parent with whom the child is with that evening would be the appropriate parent to purchase these supplies, while both parents continue efforts to teach your child the importance of planning ahead.

Which supplies should be duplicated at both homes?

In addition to the supplies listed above, educational games, flash-cards, and books/magazines on your child's reading level would enrich your child's educational growth. Your child's teacher can recommend specific selections which you can purchase or borrow from your local library. If your child's teacher expects textbooks to remain at home and your child spends his/her school week at both homes, special arrange-ments need to be discussed at the beginning of the school year. If it is not possible for the school to supply a duplicate set of textbooks, con-sider taking the time to duplicate only the pages needed for the week. While this is a tedious task, it might make the difference in your child's ability to complete homework and studying if alternating homes during the school week.

What should our child be expected to do to keep track of school sup-plies?

Your child is responsible for notifying parents of needed school supplies, taking care of supplies and replenishing supplies such as pa-per and pencils/pens regularly.

How can we help teach our child responsibility for managing school supplies?

Both parents should take the responsibility of looking through your child's backpack in elementary school on a daily basis depend-ing upon whose home the child is spending their school week with. Organization of supplies, papers, homework and classwork should be taught and reinforced daily until your child demonstrates respon-sibility to manage this on their own. Many children in middle school are still learning this skill and continue to require assistance from their parents.

"Susan's School Supply Tsunami – Oops!"

Susan's fifth grade teacher, Ms. Becker, directed the students in her class to take out their graph paper for math. Susan was so embarrassed that she did not have any for the fourth day in a row; she just wanted to crawl under the table. Even though math was her best subject and her grandfather proudly boasted that she was a math whiz, Susan was beginning to hate math. Last night when she spent the evening at her dad's house, as she does every Wednesday evening, she hesitantly asked him to buy her graph paper. Instead of ordering her usual ice cream sundae at their favorite restaurant, Susan calculated in her head that the graph paper would cost the same amount. Her best friend, Juanita told her how much she paid for it. Susan knew how much the sundae cost since she began reading the menu amazing her dad at age four! She would not have asked at all since she knew what his answer would be, but she forgot to ask her mom on Monday, and her mom had a loud telephone fight about money with her dad on Tuesday so she didn't dare ask that night. Even though the graph paper cost the same as the sundae she didn't order, her dad said no! The same answer as always was given, and it made Susan feel just as sad as ever: "I pay your mother more than enough child support for her to buy you school supplies!" Just as Ms. Becker began to frown at Susan and sigh deeply, Juanita announced that she was holding Susan's graph paper for her and got out of her seat and brought her the entire package! Susan's silent grateful look was received by Juanita with a secret knowing smile and Susan was certain that Juanita was the angel sent from heaven to rescue her from the pain of having to live with divorced fighting parents.

"Sam's School Supply Solution – WOW!"

Sam's parents both arrived separately but at the same time for their monthly conference with his second grade teacher, Mrs. Marks. Sam had been behind grade level in reading at the beginning of the school year but was rapidly making progress by reading fifteen minutes every evening and working with a reading tutor twice a week. On Wednesdays, the evening Sam was spending with his dad, his dad would pick him up from school and bring him to the tutor at the community center recommended by Mrs. Marks. His mom took him there on Mondays every week. His mom and his dad bought identical books from the used bookstore to keep at their two homes and he was reading to each of them on his nights at each of their homes. The new list of books given to both parents to purchase finally had a 2.1 on the back. Sam could hardly contain his excitement because he knew that he was reading a second grade book! Once when another student in his class teased him about the 1 on the back of his book, Sam knew he was stupid. But both his mom and his Dad promised him that they would do everything they could to help him improve his reading, if he tried his hardest. Everyone kept up their part of the bargain. But it still wasn't fair - his best buddy in class, Joseph, didn't need a reading tutor and he was in the highest reading group! When he asked his mom why, she said that everyone was very good at something and reminded Sam that he was a great artist. His dad said the same thing and also reminded Sam that he was the best joke teller. Now that Sam was reading second grade books, he wondered if he could find a joke book to read to each of his parents.

---

*Important points to remember about your child's school supplies

Purchasing school supplies is a ritual at the beginning of each school year which promotes a sense of a new beginning full of hope for a successful school year. Replenishing supplies throughout the year provides further encouragement of success for children at all grade levels. Teachers often support and reward responsibility for school supplies by giving extra credit or removing points for students not having pencils, pens, paper, etc. Compromising your child's sense of confidence and success in school is not worth making a point to your ex about fair and equitable financial arrangements. The tedious arrangements needed to provide duplicate supplies and resources at both homes are invaluable in contributing to your child's sense of confidence and success in his/her school career. Your child will also recognize that both parents value their education and will support their school career in every possible way, despite not being married to each other.

Chapter Two

Textbooks: Tornados or Touchdowns

Should our child have a duplicate set of textbooks at each home?
If your child spends school nights alternating at both homes, it would be much easier to have a duplicate set of textbooks at each home. Even if your child spends only weekends at one parent's home, there is an advantage to having a second set of textbooks there. Schoolwork can be a chore and even stressful for the child and all family members. Anything to reduce the stress would provide more encouragement for a successful school career for your child.

Will the school supply a duplicate set of textbooks?
Some schools provide a set of textbooks to be left at home for reference, studying and homework. This eliminates the heavy load in the backpack which physicians have found to contribute to spinal problems for children. Most schools do not have a budget which allows a second set of textbooks to be given to children who live in two homes, however, it is worth explaining your situation and asking your child's school.

Where can we find textbooks on our own?
Ask your child's school for assistance in locating textbooks. Sometimes, it is permissible to photocopy pages one unit or chapter at a time, in order to ensure your child has the material at both homes.

Which parent should pay for the second set, if we have to purchase them?
Discuss with your ex (out of earshot of your child) equitable arrangements for sharing the expense of a second set of textbooks. While

there is no correct way or precedent here, it is worth compromising what you might believe to be financially fair in order to provide your child with extra encouragement and convenience in completing homework and studying for tests.

Who should pay for lost or damaged textbooks?

Your child is responsible for taking care of his/her textbooks. If they become damaged or lost due to your child's not having learned that responsibility, it is your responsibility as parents to teach your child to be more responsible with his/her textbooks. It would be a good idea to assign your child a set of extra chores (at both parents' home) so that the money to replace the textbooks can be earned.

What is our child's responsibility for school textbooks?

Your child is responsible to handle textbooks carefully, not bend or write in the pages, keep track of where his/her textbooks are kept in both homes and school, and return them in good condition to the school at the end of the school year. Some schools request that textbooks be covered with book covers which can be purchased or made from brown grocery bags. Many schools have a policy which will prevent a student from graduating if textbooks are not returned or paid for.

How can we help our child keep track of their own textbooks between homes?

If possible, obtain a second copy of textbooks to be maintained at both homes. If your child will need to bring his/her textbooks home daily, arrange a special friendly reminder when making visitation arrangements. Younger children will need to have both parents assist with the transfer of textbooks when clothing and other essential are packed. Older children can be encouraged to assume responsibility for their own belongings including textbooks.

"Tom's Textbook Tornado – Oops!"

Tom was all set to study for his history exam the next day at school while spending his usual weekend with his dad. They put off studying until Sunday, since Saturday had always been fun time between father and son, even when his parents were married. Now that he was in middle school, his father offered to discontinue the Saturday ritual, but Tom said "No Way!" he really loved exploring the city with his dad and looked forward to it each weekend. He was worried about his history exam though since he only earned a "D" last quarter. He promised his mom that he would study for the exam at his dad's house over the weekend. "Oh, NO!!!" Tom realized he forgot his history book at his mom's house. He meant to pack it but his mom was rushing him to go out the door and get into his dad's car when his dad arrived to pick him up on Friday night. She didn't want to see or speak to Tom's dad. Although it had been almost five years since they were divorced, Tom's knew his mother hated his dad, since she never missed an opportunity to remind him of the awful way his dad left her after the awful way he treated her during their marriage. Tom remembers lots of fights but tried to go outside or to a friend's house when his parents used to fight so he would not have to hear it. He loved his dad and really didn't like to hear his mom constantly making mean remarks about him, but found it best over the years not to defend his dad – it just got him into more trouble with his mom. Now that they were not talking at all, at least there was no fighting to listen to. Tom wanted to call his mom and ask her to bring the history book to his dad's house, but he knew she would not be home. If he called her cell number from his dad's house, she would not answer, since she did not want to take the chance of speaking to his dad. His mom lived a half hour away, maybe he could ask his dad to drive him there, but his mom made it clear she did not want his dad anywhere near her home, unless he was picking Tom up or dropping him off. Besides, he didn't have his key – he was not allowed to bring it to his dad's house. What did she think – that his dad would steal his key in the middle of the night and make a copy of it – then sneak in when she was not home and do what?! Tom wanted to call Isaac, his best friend at school and borrow his textbook, but he was too embarrassed to explain to Isaac about how his divorced parents treated each other. He could not explain it to his history teacher either – he was sure he would not understand. Tom was feeling really bad, but he was not sure what he felt worse about – not having his history textbook to study for the test or having divorced parents that didn't talk to each other.

"Tina's Textbook Touchdown- WOW!"

Tina's fourth grade teacher explained apologetically to her parents that there just were not enough textbooks to provide a set to send home, let alone a second set for her to keep at both parents' homes. They would have to work out something to make sure that the textbooks went back and forth so that all homework could be completed and turned in daily for a large part of her grade. Tina was very worried about remembering to bring her books back and forth and was afraid that she would not be able to keep track of it. Actually, since her parents divorce last year, Tina was very worried about a lot of things lately – school grades, friends, and will boys think she is pretty? Her parents and grandparents always told her she was pretty, but how did they know what boys her age thought – it was definitely different! Just as she was wondering if Tony, who sits next to her thought she was pretty, her mom came to her room with a really cool light pink canvas bag with her name on it! It had flowers and hearts in lavender, her second favorite color (light pink was her favorite) with the words: SCHOOL BOOKS written in cursive also in lavender! Mom explained that she and dad had it made up especially for her to help all three of them remember to bring her school books back and forth between two homes. Tina's mom explained that the bag was her idea, the colors were her dad's idea and they both paid for it, having ordered it on the internet and it just arrived in the mail. Tina called her dad immediately to thank him and let him know how much she loved it. Her dad said it was designed by her mom, who always had a great artistic flair. Tina wondered why her parents got divorced if her dad really liked her mom's artistic talent, but she was getting old enough to understand that there was more to keeping a marriage together. The bag helped Tina remember most of the time, but she still forgot her textbooks sometimes and her parents also forgot to remind her sometimes. When that happened, they had a halfway meeting point where both mom and dad drove to exchange textbooks and sometimes school uniform or her favorite stuffed animal, Kookie, who Tina still slept with. She loved her mom, her dad, her cool textbook bag, school and Kookie and even started to think that maybe the boys did really find her pretty!

8

Important points to remember about your child's textbooks

It is the task of both parents to instill a sense of responsibility in their children for taking care of their possessions, including school textbooks. This responsibility may take years for a child to learn, therefore, parents need to be persistent and patient. Take the time, as Tina's parents did to find creative ways to teach this responsibility for your child's developing sense of pride and accomplishment. Avoid allowing your bitter feelings towards your ex to overpower opportunities to assist your child in being successful in school. It is worth the compromise when you see the sense of pride and confidence your child develops.

Chapter Three

Assignment Book: Blizzards or Bonanza

*What is an assignment book and why is our child expected to keep one?

An assignment book, also referred to as the daily planner, is a child's version of an adult appointment book and is used to record homework assignments, test dates, projects and other important notes to remember about school. Most schools print their own with the school logo, staff names and telephone numbers as well as the calendar of days off and testing schedule. This is a school wide endeavor, helping your child feel a connection to their school. Your child is not expected to be able to remember all homework assignments so the assignment book is an opportunity to become responsible for writing down homework and test dates.

*What should our child be writing in the assignment book?

Your child should be recording all homework assignments as instructed by the teachers. Most teachers will remind students to write in their assignment book daily, depending upon the grade level. Test dates, field trips, projects and notes home should also be recorded.

*Should our child bring the assignment book home daily?

Your child should bring the assignment book to school and home each day.

*What should we look for each day in the assignment book?

Parents should look at the assignment book to be sure that their child is recording homework assignments daily and completing the assigned homework each evening. Note days off, testing days, field trips and notes home. Sometimes teachers will expect a parent signature to assure homework was completed and checked.

Should both sets of parents be checking the assignment book?

Both sets of parents should be checking the assignment book regularly and maintain an ongoing dialogue with your child about homework assignments as well as monitoring completion. The level of monitoring will vary according to the grade level, the expectations of your child's teacher and the individual needs of your particular child.

If a parent signature is required, which parent should sign?

If a parent signature is required, the parent with whom the child is spending the night should sign the assignment book. A daily parent signature is often an intervention utilized for children who frequently forget to do homework assignments. Both parents, however, should read and monitor the assignment book for notes from the teacher and to demonstrate your interest in your child's schoolwork.

What if the assignment book gets left at one parent's home or gets lost?

Both parents should make every effort to recognize and acknowledge the importance of the assignment book by reminding their child to keep it with them when traveling from school to each of their homes. A plan should be discussed ahead of time as to how to manage any and all items left behind. A lost assignment book should be replaced as soon as possible. Many schools will provide the first one at no charge but require a fee to replace lost assignment books.

What is our child's responsibility regarding the assignment book?

Your child is responsible to develop the habit of recording all homework assignments in their assignment book, as well as any test dates and important items to remember to take care of such as field trip forms. Your child is also responsible to develop the habit of bringing the assignment book to school daily as well as bringing it home each evening.

11

How can we help our child make the best use of the assignment book?

You can encourage and monitor your child's use of their assignment book, and compare it to your own daily planner for the appointments you keep track of. Messages between the teacher and parents daily can be recorded in the assignment book when your child is struggling to achieve an educational or behavioral goal. For example, some teachers will record daily whether your child followed all classroom rules if classroom behavior needs improvement.

"Bettina's Assignment Book Blizzard – Oops!"

Even though she was in high school, Bettina was having difficulty remembering her homework assignments. She knew her ADD (Attention Deficit Disorder) made it more difficult to remember to do her homework assignments, but she was also having difficulty remembering to record them daily in her assignment book. She promised both of her parents and all five of her teachers she would try harder, but Bettina was beginning to hate even looking at her assignment book. The comments written by both of her divorced parents to her teachers made them sound like children telling on each other – it was so embarrassing! Bettina's mother wrote to the math teacher that homework was not completed since Bettina was at her dad's house on Wednesday evenings. Bettina's dad wrote that her science project had not been started because Bettina's mother had not purchased the supplies over the weekend. And this was just one week's worth of comments – Bettina was so humiliated, she wanted to crawl under a desk as she watched her teachers – all of her teachers read these notes! School was the one place she could just be a teenager and not be reminded of her parents divorce. Now that their ongoing battle was being carried out weekly in her assignment book, Bettina was even more distracted at school than before. But she knew it was her problem to fix, and that she really could not depend upon her parents for help since their problems with each other were far greater than any problems she had in school or life.

"Blair's Assignment Book Bonanza – WOW!"

Blair's mom produce two colored pens, one green and one pink, when Blair proudly brought home his first assignment book in second grade. She explained that the green pen was for his dad to sign with and the pink pen was for her to sign her name. She explained to Blair that an assignment book was like being a grown up with an appointment calendar and he had to take good care of it and remember to take it to school and both his mom's and dad's house throughout the school week each day. When Blair completed the homework assignment he had recorded in his assignment book as instructed by his teacher, his mom signed her name in pink with a heart next to it. His dad signed his name in green with a happy face next to it. Blair's classmates were even jealous of his assignment book! One boy said he was worried when his parents were getting a divorce like Blair's did last year, but Blair reassured him that having two homes could be kinda cool at times. He didn't even mind when Mrs. Brooks gave out homework, since he got to write it in his assignment book which made him feel very grown up, and got more hearts and happy faces in his book when he completed the assignments at home. He had been secretly counting them and was so excited because by the end of tonight after he finishes his spelling homework at his dad's house, he will have 20 green happy faces!! He knows that he spends more time at his mom's house because he already has 42 hearts!!!! Maybe he can get extra hearts and happy faces if he reads an extra book this weekend.

> **Important points to remember about your child's assignment book*
>
> Your child's assignment book is a recording of their homework and overall school progress. Make every effort to show a positive interest in the assignment book and record positive comments. Your child's school success is impacted by your positive attitude and interest in their assignment book. Help them learn to take pride and responsibility in this useful tool.

Chapter Four

Homework: Hurricanes or Home Runs

Whose home should our child do their homework at?

By doing their homework at both parent's homes, regardless of the amount of time spent at each home, both parents will be demonstrating the importance of education. In addition, both parents will be aware of the work your child is doing in school as well as their strengths, challenges, goals and progress.

How will we know what our child's homework assignments are?

Generally, schools provide an assignment book for children to record all homework assignments. An assignment book can be purchased at an office supply store if one is not provided by the school, or an ordinary notebook can be used to record all homework assignments. Some teachers will provide a syllabus at the beginning of the school year, depending upon the grade level.

What if my visits interfere with homework time?

It would be best to include homework time during your visits with your child. Each parent has a responsibility to monitor and encourage a successful school career. Your role is to inspire, guide and mentor their education; your children are not guests who you are responsible to entertain.

How do we know if our child turned in all homework assignments?

Your child's teacher will inform you at the beginning of the school year what the policy is for remaining in contact and the expectations of parents in monitoring your child's homework completion. Report cards, interim reports, progress reports, daily homework assignment book and parent teacher conferences are some ways for you to be informed.

How much help should we give our child with their homework?

The appropriate amount of help with homework given to your child will depend upon the grade level and their ability. Help can be in the form of encouragement, support, monitoring, time and space management and companionship. Each teacher will have a different expectation from parents regarding homework, but most wish to see what the child knows how to do on their own, without major assistance from parents.

Which parent is responsible for making sure homework is completed?

While homework completion is the responsibility of both parents, it is more realistic for the parent with whom the child is spending the night to monitor the completed homework due the next day. Homework assignments requiring several days, studying for tests and completing major projects will require communication between both parents in order to monitor, unless the child is old enough or mature enough to monitor his/her own work.

What is our child's responsibility regarding homework?

Your child is responsible for recording the daily homework assignments in his/her assignment book, bringing home the necessary books, papers and notes in order to complete the assignments, letting parents know what the assignments are, completing the assignments to the best of their ability and handing in all homework assignments on time.

How can we help our child in completing all homework?

Some children develop motivation on their own at an early age while others struggle with motivation to complete homework. If your child is struggling with motivation, you may wish to consider developing a reward plan, or set up logical consequences. See your child's school Guidance Counselor for assistance in finding age appropriate rewards and consequences.

"Howard's Homework Hurricane – Oops!"

Howard's dad picked him up on Friday evening for their usual weekend together and he could not wait! As soon as his dad arrived, Howard put away his reading and math books, grabbed his baseball mitt, his fishing pole and his favorite videogames. His mom wanted him to bring his reading book to catch up with the class since he was behind in reading and his math book to practice since he was almost failing math. "No way!" protested Howard, time with his dad was a vacation from school. His mom wished she could do fun things with Howard too, and tried to explain to his dad how important the fourth grade was, but Howard's dad insisted that he didn't get to spend enough time with his son and did not want to spoil their time with schoolwork. His mom wanted to tell him that she wished that she and Howard could have fun together sometimes instead of always doing schoolwork, but she knew that her ex-husband just didn't value education the same way she did and he was unrealistic about his son's abilities. "He'll be fine when he gets older, elementary school grades don't count", Howard's dad insisted. His mom wished that he would not continually say that in front of Howard since Howard began repeating this same statement every evening when she tried to get him to do his homework. Now Wednesday evenings, after dinner with his dad, it became impossible to complete homework. She knew that if she gave up and let him fail the grade, Howard would feel terrible about himself and regret it. That would certainly teach his dad a lesson and might get him to support homework and Howard's education. She realized, however, that teaching her ex-husband a lesson at the expense of her son's feelings would not be satisfying. She wanted the best for Howard and promised herself she would be persistent and find a way to help him become more motivated, with or without his father's encouragement. Maybe the new math computer game she found at the library will interest him.

"Helena's Homework Home Run – WOW!"

Helena was about to ask her mom for help with her algebra assignment when she remembered that her mother didn't know algebra. Instead she asked if her mom would take her to her dad's house that evening so he could help her with her math. Helena's dad was an accountant and math was his best subject. Even though it was Tuesday night, one of her nights at her mom's house, she knew her mom would not mind. At the beginning of high school, her mom and dad had a family meeting and told her they would be getting divorced. Helena had mixed feelings, although she was sad, her parents explained that she would be spending almost equal time at both their homes and they would be flexible with the schedule depending upon her school and social plans. She knew that both her parents valued her education and would be supportive of anything related to school, but she was surprised and relieved to hear that they understood how important her friends were to her as well. In the two years since the divorce, Helena's parents kept their word one hundred percent! Anytime Helena needed help with math or science, she went to her dad's house, even when she was scheduled to spend the night with her mom. And the week her dad's computer was out of service, she spent the entire week at her mom's so she could complete her research project for English and hand it in on time. Besides, her mom was better at checking her grammar and offering ideas for her writing. Helena just wished her mom and dad did not have to do so much driving for her. They were always transporting her back and forth between homes, sometimes just to get a book she forgot at one home. They never even complained about it, although she knew how tiring it was. She could not wait to get her driver's license and drive herself! They also promised she could get her license if she kept up her grades, did all her homework and studied hard for her exams. Helena kept up her part of the bargain and was expecting to be on the honor roll this semester and she knew that she had her parents to thank for that!

Important points to remember about your child's homework

Homework is given by teachers in order to reinforce and practice the material learned in school. In addition, it helps children develop habits, routines and responsibility. A positive and supportive attitude from both parents regarding homework will promote a positive educational career for your child and help instill responsibility for their schoolwork.

17

Exams/Tests/Quizzes: Earthquakes or Epic

How will we know when there are quizzes, tests and exams?

Your child's teacher will inform you at the beginning of the school year how often and generally when exams are given. Your child is expected to keep track of exam dates in their assignment book as well. Some teachers, usually in later grades, provide a syllabus, in which all exam dates as well as homework assignments are listed at the beginning of the school year. In elementary school, it is often the custom to have a weekly spelling test on Fridays, for example. Quizzes can either be announced ahead of time or given without notice, a practice known as "pop quizzes." Many schools have instituted an online webpage where test dates as well as homework assignments are listed.

Which parent should help our child study for tests?

Ideally, both parents should help their child study for tests. The majority of studying should not be left for the night before the test, as most children's best learning style is by repetition. Some helpful study guides are often provided by the teacher, as well as a recommendation to place facts on index cards, or review questions at the end of each chapter in the text.

Should I skip a visit with my child if there is an important test the next day?

Unless you are unable to provide an appropriate study time and atmosphere for your child or are unable to help with the subject matter, there is no reason to skip a scheduled visit. Many parents include study time in the car or at a restaurant. If the driving time to and from your

18

home is too great a distance, you may wish to take your child to a local public library to assist and monitor study time.

How much time should be spent studying for exams?

The amount of time needed to study for exams varies widely according to each child's individual abilities and learning style. Your child's teacher will provide a typical suggested amount of time; however, your child's needs may vary widely from the average. It is important as a parent to become familiar with your child's learning styles so you may be of the greatest possible assistance in studying.

How can we find out what grade my child received on the test?

Teachers generally return completed and graded tests to their students for their review. Many schools have developed an online website where you may check your child's test grades as well as homework completion and overall progress.

What if our child needs extra help studying?

Many children have difficulty learning the study techniques which work best for them. Your child's teacher is the best source of ideas of the various study skills available for your child. Local libraries, high schools and private facilities offer tutoring programs which your child's school Guidance Counselor can direct you towards.

How can we help our child study for tests?

You can help you child study for tests by developing a daily routine which involves studying, in addition to completing homework. Fun games and routines can also be established as part of your time together. Most importantly, however, is to become acquainted with your child's best learning style so you may be supportive in a manor that is the least threatening and frustrating for your child. Your child's teacher is the best resource for specific target materials for each subject.

What are statewide standardized tests and what do the scores mean?

All states have a standardized testing program which determines your child's progress from year to year and standing among others in their grades level. Some states require a minimum passing score to be

19

promoted to the next grade, or to qualify for registration in special programs or classes. Some states provide extra money to school districts where an increase in student achievement is evidenced by standardized test scores. Teacher bonuses have been earned based upon standardized test scores as well in certain school districts. Depending upon the state, there may be a strong emphasis on statewide standardized tests, with additional tutoring offered after school and on weekends.

How can children make sure they study properly for their exams?

Monitoring your child's study schedule and techniques will be more time intensive in earlier grades, and with children having special learning needs such as learning disabled or ADHD. As they get older and demonstrate more independence as well as good grades, it will be less necessary for parents to monitor and assist with their child's studying. Test grades as well as teacher conferences will be your guide as to the needs of your child, which may change as they progress through their school career, and depending upon their strengths and challenges.

How can we help encourage our child to take responsibility for studying?

Parents can encourage their children to develop good study habits by including studying as a daily routine from early on in their school career. Providing a comfortable location free from distractions, being consistent and sometimes keeping them company with your own "studying" will set a positive role model for future years.

"Eva's Exam Earthquake – Oops!"

Eva's school district was having statewide testing for the entire week and Eva could not focus! She was in all advanced classes for seventh grade and had been her entire school career, but today her mind was racing with thoughts of court. Her mom explained to her that her dad was suing her in court for child custody. He really did not want to raise her, according to her mom, but just wanted to stop paying child support. "It was all about the money!" Eva kept hearing over and over again in her head. But her dad told her a different story – according to him, Eva's mom didn't use the money wisely, always getting her nails done and buying expensive shoes for herself – never spending the money for Eva, as dictated by the courts. Besides, she was not fit to raise a teenage girl, with all the boyfriends she had since the two years her parents were divorced, according to her dad. He even told Eva that her mom had boyfriends throughout their marriage, a concept that Eva did not believe mostly. It was 10:00 AM and at this moment the judge could be deciding the fate of her life! It was unfair that she did not get to have a say, even though Eva was not sure what she wanted. She was, however, relieved that she did not need to say who she preferred to live with because either parent would have hurt feelings. Her school Guidance Counselor recommended that she tell her parents that it was not fair to put her in the middle of their fight. They listened to her but always went back to their old ways of trying to convince her that the other parent was wrong. If only they knew how much it hurt her..."Time is up, put down your pencils, close your test booklet", the announcement came over the loudspeaker. Eva closed her test booklet, but could not remember if she completed the exam.

Ely's Exam Epic – "WOW!"

Ely watched with glee as his father was drawing a funny hat with feathers and balloons on the H A T letters of the word hat on the placemat in their favorite restaurant. Even though Ely was only six years old and at the beginning of the first grade, he knew he loved homework time with his dad! Every Thursday evening, Ely's dad took him out to dinner and studied his spelling words with him. Each week, he made up a funny story, picture or joke and Ely could not wait to see what his dad had in mind for the other nine words. They used to go out every Wednesday evening in the two years since his parents were divorced, but his Dad's work schedule changed so Ely's day changed to Thursday evenings. Ely did not know the truth, which was that his sister's counseling appointment was on Thursday evenings and having Ely around was distracting during that time. His mom could not help him study for his spelling test on that night as she was very anxious about his sister's "teenage" problems, so his mom and dad developed the plan of spelling test studying with dad at dinner and Ely loved it! He got a

90% or 100% each week on his exams, although once his teacher had to remind him not to draw pictures on his test paper!

---

*Important points to remember about your child's exams

Early identification of your child's best learning style, study routines, providing a quiet study location and parent monitoring are crucial in developing good study habits for your child. Frequent checking with your child's teacher(s) and seeking additional tutoring may be necessary for problem situations. Try to be creative, make studying fun and cooperate with your ex for coordinating your child's best study practices.

Chapter Six

Projects: Pitfalls or Pleasures

*Why do teachers assign projects?

Projects are assigned by teachers in order to reinforce the material that is learned in school and bring a culmination to a themed unit. In addition, teachers recognize the various learning styles of their students and projects are assigned to address these learning styles. For example, experiential and tactile learners will absorb the material being presented after building a collage representing an aspect of the unit. Focusing on multiple learning styles also reinforces learning for all students. Another skill being learned is organization strategies, as many projects are assigned months in advance and require multiple steps. Some projects require working with other students in a group, another important skill which teaches students how to compromise and share their resources.

*What major projects are generally assigned throughout the grades?

Book reports and poster board projects are common in early grades, with science and social studies projects common for older grades. High school students are often assigned research reports, interviewing and community service projects.

*How will we know when a project is assigned to our child?

At the beginning of the school year, the teacher will generally let parents know at an open house or an introductory letter the projects that will be assigned throughout the school year. High school teachers usually present students with a syllabus describing all assignments, test dates, homework and projects throughout the school year.

Which parent should work with the child on the project?

Either or both parents can work with their child on school projects; however joint custody parents will need to communicate closely for their elementary school age children in coordinating assistance in completing projects. Where the child spends their school nights and weekends will need to be considered as well as the organizational and technical skills of each parent. Neither parent should feel that it is not their responsibility.

Which parent should pay for the supplies needed for the project?

Schools do not expect parents to pay large amounts of money for supplies, instead expect children to use typical household materials found in the home. In addition, schools can sometimes supply the special materials needed if the parents have difficulty affording extras for their child. Do not be shy about asking. Joint custody parents should discuss with each other and negotiate ahead of time who will pay for any extra supplies. Projects can be stressful for your children; they do not need the additional worry about parents arguing about who is responsible for the cost of the supplies.

Which parent should help drive the project to school if needed?

The parent's home where the child is going to school the morning the project is due would be the most appropriate joint custody parent to help transport the project to school. While it may seem trivial, your child's pride in handing in the culmination of their hard work, as well as their responsibility in protecting the project during transport is a joy to observe and an opportunity to teach your children the positive feelings involved with completing a difficult project.

How much help should our child need on special projects?

Your child should be assisted in developing a time schedule for long term projects as well as monitoring their compliance with their schedule. Depending upon their age and ability, children may require assistance in selecting a project theme if not assigned, technical assistance, research assistance, proof reading, editing and frequent praise. Your child's teacher will appreciate a project completed primarily by your child more than parent completed projects which may look attractive and neat but clearly not done by your child.

*Which parent gets to keep the project after it is returned?

Sometimes the joint custody parent, who spent many months monitoring, supporting and assisting with their child's project, feels a special attachment to the project as a symbol of the work completed together. The project, however, belongs to your child and (s)he should decide where it should be kept after being returned from the school. If the project is an art project, it will give your child a great sense of self esteem if the project is displayed in your home.

*What is our child's responsibility regarding school projects?

Your child is responsible to let both parents know well in advance when a project is assigned, what materials will be needed, and when it is due. Your child is also responsible to develop a timeline with your help for completing the project and working to the best of their ability until the project is completed.

*How can we help our child learn to take responsibility for their school projects?

Both joint custody parents will need to work diligently in instilling the importance of completing school projects with their children. This will involve frequent monitoring of the steps involved toward completion as well as coordinating, cooperating and communicating with each other throughout the steps along the way.

"Peter's Project Pitfall – Oops!"

Peter's third grade teacher assigned the first monthly book report for the school year and Peter was worried. He never did a book report before. His teacher gave them three weeks to complete the report. He had to write the title of the book, the author, the main characters, the setting, a summary of the story and the ending. He also had to include his favorite part. Then, he had to present his report to the class, out loud in front of the classroom! He was worried about presenting in front of the class – maybe the other students would laugh at him. He knew that he could ask his mom for help – she would understand his worry and always encouraged and calmed him. Peter was afraid to explain his book report to his dad; his dad got angry often and yelled a lot. Even though one time his dad explained that he was not yelling at Peter, Peter always got nervous and worried when his dad yelled. That evening, he was at his dad's, as he always was on Wednesday evenings since his parents had gotten a divorce two years ago. His dad was talking on the telephone to his uncle and was yelling loudly as usual. He heard his dad curse and call his mother names but tried to just read his book for his book report. Peter couldn't remember what he read because he couldn't stop thinking about his dad yelling. That night he tried to ask his dad to read to him before bed and show him his book and book report, but his dad quickly put him to bed and left the room. The yelling began again and this time it was a telephone conversation to his best friend and there was more name calling about his mom. Peter got too upset to sleep and dropped his reading book but was too afraid to get out of bed to pick it up. In the morning, he forgot about his book when he was getting ready for school. His dad was in a good mood and cooked him a great breakfast – pancakes – his favorite! He even forgot about the yelling last night, his dad was really a fun guy after all. Peter forgot about his book report and when he did remember, he forgot where he left his book. When he told his mother about it, she suggested that he call his dad and ask him to look for it at his home. He did and his dad said he would but must have forgotten because he didn't call Peter back. Two weeks later Peter found his reading book at his dad's house under his bed and began reading it again. He had only two days to finish the book and write the report. Maybe his dad could ask his teacher for an extension and explain the lost book. He was with his dad for the weekend and could finish the book and write the report if he tried really hard. But his dad was very excited about the football game on Sunday and was having his brother and friend over for the game on his big screen new HD television. Peter was interested in football and wanted to be part of the guy party so he forgot all about the book report. On Monday when the teacher asked him for his book report, he was the only one who did not hand it in. Peter wanted to blame his dad for not finding his book when he lost it and for watching the football game instead of helping him with his report, but he knew it was really his own fault.

"Paola's Project Pleasure – WOW!"

Paola's dad reluctantly agreed to help her with her science project, trying not to sound too disinterested, as he was already given a heads-up by his ex-wife that Paola was going to ask him for help. Since his parents had owned a nursery while he was growing up, Paola decided that an experiment with different types of soil would be fun for the two of them to do each weekend she was visiting with him, which was every other weekend since her parents divorced three years ago. Paola tried so hard to find activities that interested her dad since he seemed unable to think of fun things to do with a thirteen year old girl. She could understand that, but surely he would be interested in growing plants. Her mother sent over three decorative flower pots that she was not using and a list of websites for Paola and her father to explore together. As they began searching the computer, Paola's dad thought about the nursery his parents used to own and how he truly enjoyed visiting it and even had his first job there. These were pleasing thoughts since his parents had both passed away when Paola was very young. Even though she could not remember them, Paola felt that she was beginning to know her grandparents as her father told lively stories of the fun they had while he was growing up. He also began to realize that helping Paola with her science project actually could be fun after all and was looking forward to seeing which seedlings grew best in the various soil types they planted them in. Paola's dad added two more flower pots since there were five soil combinations they decided to try. When it was time to write up the science project on the project board that Paola's mom sent over, along with craft supplies to do the lettering and borders, her dad just watched, since he explained that he was "craft challenged" and continued to regal Paola with stories of his parents. After all, she was supposed to do the project herself, he rationalized. Finally, Paola's dad was ready to drive the project to school with her one Monday AM, when he realized it would not fit in his new snazzy two seater sports car. Frantic, he called Paola's mom who agreed to arrange coverage at work and drive the project to school with her SUV while Paola's dad followed behind to help Paola carry the project to her classroom. It was a good thing Paola's mom showed up, because she brought two sided tape with her to help fasten the lettering that kept falling off the project board. The teacher was very impressed and re-marked that it could win a chance to be in the county science fair competition. Paola's father could not be more proud! The project actually did take second place in her school and was a finalist in the county competition, a success that Paola and her dad talked about the entire year.

The following year, Paola's dad announced his engagement to Eva, a lady he had been dating for a while on the same weekend Paola was about to ask him to help her with her science project again. She asked anyway, even though she suspected that her father would no longer be interested. To her surprise, not only was he excited about it, but it turned out he had several ideas including more planting and something about magnets. Paola turned to look at Eva, expected her to disapprove and she could not have been more relieved when Eva announced that she had to visit both her mom and dad separately that day and would be home late. It turned out that her parents were divorced too and Eva said it was fine growing up with divorced parents because her parents got along with each other. Eva did come home late, but called to say that she ordered a pizza and had left out a coupon for Pizza Pizzazo for Paola and her dad for dinner. When Eva did arrive home, she brought the newest teen video release that Paola was dying to see, caramel pop-corn, Paola's favorite, and a small bag from a craft store. When Paola opened it up, she found three brand new rolls of two sided tape. Paola politely remarked that she was sure only her mother knew her favorite things and what she needed for her science project and Eva agreed by responding that she had phoned Paola's mom for some clues.

---

*Important points to remember about your child's projects

School projects are an ideal means to teach your child responsi-bility, time management, increase their sense of self esteem and have fun together. Joint custody parents have a unique opportunity to sup-port these qualities during their visits if it is well planned out and supported by both parents.

Chapter Seven

Returned Papers and Tests: Roadblocks or Raves

What should parents do with all the papers that have been graded and returned?

It is a good idea to keep all returned school papers filed at home according to quarter and subject for the entire school year. They will be good reference for studying for tests and evaluating your child's progress. On occasion, a teacher forgets to record grade in their grade book and will correct this mistake when you produce returned paper.

How does second custodial parent see our child's graded school papers?

Ask your child to show you all of his/her graded returned papers before storing them at the home chosen for storing them. Discuss the importance of your involvement with your child's school progress with your ex spouse to encourage them to show you the returned papers as well.

Which parent should sign schoolwork to be returned to the teacher?

It is permissible for either or both joint custody parents to sign papers required to be signed by a parent and returned to school, however, both parents should see all school papers in order to best support your child's academic goals and progress.

Is it okay for parents to look in our child's backpack?

It is recommended that you check your child's back pack regularly, especially elementary school children, as they are still developing the responsibility of monitoring their school work. Older children may resent the lack of privacy and feel that you are distrusting them; however, both parents are in a position to explain the importance of parental monitoring and assistance with school.

*Whose responsibility is it to insure each parent sees returned school papers?

The responsibility to ensure that both parents see returned school papers belongs to both joint custody parents and their children equally.

*What should I do if my ex doesn't show me our child's schoolwork?

The spirit of joint custody is for both parents to take part in important aspects of your child's life, including school. By providing encouragement and support toward your child's school goals and progress, as well as participating in their school events, you will be demonstrating a genuine interest in your child's academic success and will be less likely to encounter resistance. As a last resort, you may wish to meet with your child's teacher in order to periodically view his/her work. Your school's Guidance Counselor may be able to mediate this academic situation between joint custody parents.

*What is our child's responsibility regarding returned school papers?

Your child is responsible to show their returned papers and tests to both parents and learn how to maintain a filing system at home in order to keep papers for studying or evaluating areas of needed improvement.

*How can parents help their children to be organized with schoolwork?

Parents can help their children to be organized with their school papers by providing appropriate folders and storage areas at home, working with your child daily to maintain organization and being the best possible role model they can. Usually one joint custody parent is better organized in their lives than the other regarding filing papers and it would make sense for that parent to teach and monitor their children's organization skills.

*Should our children be expected to show their schoolwork to both parents?

Children should be expected to develop the responsibility to show their schoolwork to both joint custody parents and encouraged by both parents to do so.

"Rita's Returned Papers Roadblock – Oops!"

Rita tried to find her spelling homework in her backpack but it was such a mess, it would be hard for anyone to find anything in there! At least that is what her teacher said, when she tried to help her. Ever since her parent's divorce, Rita did not take school papers out of her bag. Both of her parents treated her school papers as if they were their own and it made Rita feel invisible. Her mom would comment: "Wow, we did good work!" if Rita brought home an A on her spelling test after her mom helped her study. And her dad said that Rita would have gotten a better grade in math if she had studied for the test with him. Rita overheard her dad telling his sister that he was going to use the math homework and returned tests to prove in court that he should have custody of Rita! And once when Rita had to get a parent signature on her F grade on her history test her mother wrote on the paper that Rita was with her dad the weekend before the test and that is why she did not do well. Rita knew by now that her grades were her own responsibility and did not like her parents treating them like they were their own. She especially did not want her school papers to be used as evidence in court for a custody hearing – is that possible? She asked her teacher but he did not know and referred her to the school Guidance Counselor. But she did not have a problem – it was her parents' problem – maybe they should see the Guidance Counselor, thought Rita, just as her teacher finally announced that she had found Rita's spelling homework in a side pocket of the back pack. By then, Rita almost didn't care anymore; she was so busy thinking of how angry she was with both of her parents.

"Richard's Returned Papers Raves – WOW!"

Richard knew he was in luck when his seventh grade history teacher offered extra credit points to anyone who could bring in their notes for the entire quarter for the new student to copy. Ever since elementary school, his mom made him file all his school papers at the end of the week on Friday afternoon before going out to play. At first she helped him, and then she taught him to do it himself. Sometimes it took him only five minutes, longer than he used to complain about each week. He really didn't see why it was important until last year when he left his textbook at school over the long weekend and used his notes to study for his exam. And then there was the time he brought all his school work from elementary school to his dad's house to show his grandmother his schoolwork. She used to be a teacher in South America and was going to be visiting with his dad for a whole month. Richard thought it was a dumb idea but his grandmother loved poring over his papers, even from kindergarten! Since Richard's parents divorced two years ago, his grandmother spends a month with Richard and his dad on the month he stays with his dad in the summer. Richard doesn't mind since she is a great cook. She also lets Richard bring his friends from his dad's neighborhood over for dinner. This summer, his grandmother was looking forward to seeing Richard's grades and his extra credit might make the difference between a B and an A.

---

*Important points to remember about your child's returned papers

Teach your child to file his/her school papers for use later for studying and reviewing for tests. It is helpful to analyze problem areas if your child is struggling with a concept in one of their classes. An accordion type folder can be organized by subject and quarter and stored away at the end of the school year easily. Any filing system will do, as long as it is used regularly. Consult with your child's teacher as to what papers should be kept and what can be discarded. Organizations skills are difficult for many adults and cause problems with work responsibilities, paying bills and computing taxes. Early lessons in keeping papers organized will develop into later adult habits.

Chapter Eight

Progress Reports: Punishment or Purr-fect's

What are progress reports and interim reports?
Progress reports are similar to report cards in that they summarize a student's accumulated academic and behavioral progress since their last progress report. Interim reports generally are provided halfway between report cards.

Why do schools issue progress reports?
Schools issue progress reports so that students and their parents will have ongoing feedback as to the student's academic and behavioral progress in school, in order to encourage parents to take an active part in encouraging success for their child.

How often are progress reports given out?
Different schools and grades have various policies regarding progress reports. Some schools issue them only when there is a problem. Some schools advise a daily progress report for students experiencing difficulty with either academic and/or behavioral goals.

How will we know the schedule of progress reports?
At the beginning of the school year, your child's teacher will explain the purpose and schedule of progress reports. This may be found in the school handbook and is generally discussed during open house.

How can we get a copy of our child's progress report?
If your child did not bring home an expected progress report, it is wise to contact the school and inquire about the issuing of progress re-

ports. Some children will "forget" to show their progress report to their parents when they are handed out at school.

How do we interpret the progress report?

Various school districts will have different codes for reporting your child's progress. The codes are generally explained on the progress report. Common codes are:

"S": Satisfactory; "U": Unsatisfactory; "N": Needs Improvement.

How should we discuss our child's progress with him/her?

It is best to refer to problems as "challenges" and "goals" when discussing your child's progress report with them. Support and encouragement will enable a plan for improvement will occur more readily. Inquire as to their own ideas of how they can improve. Don't forget to praise positive progress.

Should we give rewards? Punishments? Ultimatums?

Your child's individual needs and your personal parenting style will dictate whether you offer rewards or consequences as opposed to praise and encouragement. Consequences can reduce your child's sense of self esteem and encourage a feeling of hopelessness for some children. It is best to be sensitive to your child's learning style and determine what works best for each individual child.

Do I have to show my ex our child's progress reports?

Most joint custody agreements call for both parents to participate in their child's educational career. Both parents need to be aware of their child's school progress in order to do their best to support their child's education, therefore, it is expected that the primary custodial parent provide a copy of all progress reports to the other participating parent, as the reports are given.

Should our child be expected to show both parents their progress report?

Your child should show a copy of his/her progress report to both parents. If your child is afraid of your reaction, your ex spouse might try to soften your reaction to your child by showing it to you first.

What if we have questions about the progress reports?
Your child's teacher and the school Guidance Department can help you understand the progress report. Do not hesitate to contact the school for a better understanding of your child's progress report and ideas of how you can best encourage improvement.

How can we help our child show responsibility regarding progress reports?
Encourage your child to bring home all progress reports and share them with both parents by explaining that you will help him/her find ways to improve if there are areas of challenge.

"Phil's Progress Report Punishment – Oops!"

Phil carefully hid his monthly progress report in his backpack since he did not want his parents to see it. He got his first F in fourth grade and was very sad about it. He almost cried when he saw it in writing, even though he already knew it was coming. The rest of the class would have seen him cry so he managed to hold back his tears. It was just so hard to memorize his spelling words each week, he would become too frustrated to study them and got an F on almost every spelling test. He got an A in science and math and everyone knew that was more important than stupid spelling. Anyway, a person could always use a dictionary – isn't that what they were for – duh! Just the same, if his father saw his F, he would hit the roof! But not as high as his mother, who said that no F's were allowed in her house. He was already spending Wednesday evenings and every other weekend with his dad, since his parents had gotten divorced just six months earlier. Would she kick him out and make him live with his dad full time? Phil would not get a chance to find out, since he had no intention of showing his mother or father his progress report. He hadn't counted on his dad looking in his backpack for a pencil later that evening and finding it. Just as he had feared, Phil's dad hit the roof! Well, he didn't really hit the roof but if words could hammer, then the roof would have definitely come down. Phil did not even get a chance to explain about how difficult it was for him to memorize spelling words, but since his parents divorce, he didn't get a chance to explain anything anymore. Both of them were always so angry at each other, it was hard to find a time to talk to either of them when they were in a good mood. Phil actually was having difficulty remembering the last time he saw either his mother or his dad in a good mood since the divorce. Now his dad was blaming his mom for his F. It was no use trying to explain anything to his dad. Next his dad was calling his mom and they got into a big fight about Phil's F. Phil wanted to say that the F was his and his own fault, it was not their grade and it was not their fault, but he was not given a chance to say anything. He was punished by his mom – grounded for a month!! That meant he would miss the opening of baseball season, something he and his dad were looking forward to. Phil was hoping to see a smile on his dad's face finally when baseball season began, but now that was not going to happen and it was his own fault – just like the divorce. Even though a counselor at school told him the divorce was not his fault, he knew it really was. His parents fought about him all the time and that is why they got a divorce. Phil knew that from the bottom of his heart, just as he knew that the F meant he was stupid and would never learn. It was useless to try anyway, since he was not going to learn the spelling words and would probably get an F on his report card. After all, Phil thought, he was a failure at spelling and a failure as a son.

"Pam's Progress Report Purr-fect – WOW!"

All five of Pam's eighth grade teachers, both her parents and her step mom sat around a small table in the school media center with the school Guidance Counselor sitting next to Pam. It was decided that she would use a daily progress report to record all of her homework assignments. Her teachers would sign that she recorded the correct assignment and her parents would sign that she completed them. If this worked, Pam would never forget a homework assignment again and her report card grades would reflect her test grades of A's and B's. Pam was hoping this would work. She felt stupid for continuing to forget to write her homework assignments down and then forgetting to do them at home. Everyone was disappointed in her, but most of all, Pam was disappointed in herself. Besides, she would never be able to get into Norcrest High School, where she hoped to apply next semester. Her older sister and bother went there and all her friends were planning on going there if they got accepted. Of course, with all A's and B's, her three best friends will certainly be accepted and Pam couldn't imagine not going to high school with them. So...everyone at the table was making a commitment to help Pam. Her dad would sign her planner every Monday and Tuesday evening, her mom would sign her planner every Wednesday and Thursday evening and her step mom would sign her planner every Friday evening. Pam was sure that the teachers would be confused by her visitation schedule, but they all understood and said they had lots of kids in their classes that lived with two families. The first week, Pam remembered to do her homework almost every night, but by the second week she completed every assignment. She even got all A's on her homework assignment and all her teachers told her they knew she could do it. Pam's parents encouraged her and praised her every night. But the person who was the most proud of her improvement was herself!

Important points to remember about your child's progress reports.

Progress reports are a perfect opportunity to teach your child cooperative problem solving. Developing a plan in cooperation with teacher and both joint custody parents to improve a situation your child is struggling with will give your child a positive experience which they can use as a life skill throughout their school and work career. Do not miss an opportunity to teach your child the importance of working toward a goal and cooperating with others to achieve a goal.

Chapter Nine

Report Cards: Ravines or Rallies

How often are report cards issued?
Most schools organize their school year in four equal quarters with a report card issued at the end of each quarter. Teachers are generally given a day to post grades and the report cards are generated by the computer and distributed between several days and several weeks after the quarter has ended.

What are the significant parts of the report card?
The report card lists grades, either in letter format or numerical format, behavior, grade level, attendance and sometimes standardized test results. There is a code to refer to and generally a note from the teacher if a conference is requested.

How are progress reports different than report cards?
Report cards are documented grades posted in your child's cumulative school file. Progress reports are previews of what the report card grades look like so far several weeks into the grading cycle, and treated in a less formal manner.

How can we get a copy of our child's report card?
Your child will be given a copy of their report card when it is issued. You may also request a copy from your child's school. Some schools make report card grades as well as progress reports available on a computer system. Both joint custodial parents are entitled to this as well as other documents in your child's school records.

How will we know if our child is in danger of not passing the grade?
Your child's teacher and/or Guidance Counselor will request a conference with parents if your child is in danger of being retained in their

current grade. Opportunities to improve performance or sign an attendance contract will be provided with an honest discussion of the positive and negative aspects of retention.

How are the grades determined on the report card?

Teachers generally present a formula at the beginning of the school year explaining what percentage of the report card grade is determined by tests, quizzes, homework, class work, participation and projects. Some other aspects included in computing the grade are organization of notebook and folder, extra credit and citizenship. Each teacher has their own formula which is generally clearly presented to both students and their parents.

What if I feel the teacher is being unfair with our child?

The best way to resolve a situation where you feel that the teacher is being unfair with your child is to have a face to face conference where you inquire as to your child's academic and behavioral performance in the teacher's classroom. You might find out information that your child did not share with you in order to avoid getting into trouble. You might also wish to inquire as to the teacher's grading policy and discipline policy. After learning why your child received the grade or consequence, reevaluate your opinion of whether or not the teacher is following a consistent policy with your child. If you feel that the treatment is unfair still, politely state your feelings with specific reference to the teacher's policy. The school Guidance Counselor, Assistant Principal or Principal would be the next step if your situation has not been resolved. Remember to stick to the facts.

Should my ex be expected to provide a copy of our child's report card to me?

It would be an act of consideration if all primary custodial parents simply made a photocopy of their child's report card to provide to the other custodial parent. Bitterness and an unwillingness to share the monitoring of their child's academic progress is less often the reason this does not occur. Many parents simply do not take the time to carry out this simple task. While this is not spelled out precisely in the joint custodial agreement, it is, however, an example of the spirit of shared custody. It is also a good example of how schools can assist parents with shared custody by providing two copies to children in this situation.

Should we discuss our child's report card with him/her?

A discussion of your child's report card with him/her should include a positive, solution oriented approach. Begin by asking your child his/her opinion of the grades and if it was an accurate reflection of their best work. Next praise any improvement or significant high grades. Finally discuss low grades as struggles and goals for improvement. Finally put a plan in place to improve areas of concern.

Should we provide rewards and incentives for good grades and punish or ground our child for low grades?

Parenting styles of discipline, rewards and consequences vary according to the beliefs of the parents and the particular needs of the child. Verbal praise early on will encourage your child to develop personal pride and motivation as they proceed through their school career more so than tangible rewards. Participating in a plan for improvement will enhance feelings of hopefulness, cultivate problem solving skills and avoid feelings of defeat children often experience with low grades.

What if both parents disagree on the use of rewards/punishments/incentives?

Married parents often disagree on parenting styles just as divorced joint custodial parents do. It is of great importance to your child's emotional development that a discussion takes place and compromise is reached. If disagreement is evident to your child, a common response is for children to manipulate the situation to their advantage. If needed, a Family Therapist can help both parties reach a compromise position on the use of rewards, punishments and consequences.

Should children show their report card and discuss it with both parents?

Children should be taught and encouraged to show all school papers including report cards to both joint custodial parents.

What is our child's responsibility regarding his/her report card?

Your child is responsible to know how report card grades are calculated, bring home a copy of the report card to show to both parents and discuss his/her school progress including goals and plans for improvement if needed.

How can we help our child learn to be responsible regarding report cards?

Parents can become familiar with the school calendar so they can remind their child the day report cards are issued and encourage their children to participate in a solution oriented discussion and assessment of their school progress.

"Rory's Report Card Ravine – Oops!"

Rory always suspected that her dad loved his new stepchildren more than he loved her, but now she had proof! He took both of them out to Pizza Pinazzo, her favorite restaurant, for dinner last weekend, one of her every other weekend visits with her mother. Ever since her parents divorced three years ago, Rory had been living with her dad and visiting her mother every other weekend and Wednesday evenings. Both her parents felt this was best since her mom traveled for her job and would not be home often to care for Rory. But why did her dad have to marry another woman with children? When it was just Rory and her dad, they went to the restaurant of her choice, and she could sit in the front seat of the car all the time. Now, her new step mom sits in the front seat and she almost never gets to spend time alone with her dad. Her new step sisters were okay and sometimes it was fun to be with them – like a sleepover with friends, but they always got all A's in school and Rory usually got C's. Even though they were older and in middle school and Rory was only in third grade, she found out that they always got A's even in elementary school too! And that is why they went out to Pizza Pinazzo without her – it was a reward for good report card grades. Dad's new wife always took her daughters out to dinner at a restaurant of their choice when they got their report cards as a reward for good grades and the tradition continued after she married Rory's dad. Rory was never included in this celebration and she suspected it was because her dad was beginning to love his stepchildren more than he loved her. After all, they were smarter than Rory, prettier and better athletes. Rory was sure that she could never be as perfect as her stepsisters no matter how hard she tried. One time Rory even tried to wear the same style of clothing as they did but her mom said she looked too grown up. She tried to watch the same TV shows but her dad said she was too young. And when she wanted to get her hair cut in the same style, her step mom said that Rory's hair was too fine and would not look good in that style. When Rory was sure her dad didn't think she was good enough and decided to hide her report card so he would not see the C's, her step mom found it in her backpack and showed it to her dad. He did not comment on the grades one single bit, even though she brought her math grade up to a C+, the highest ever for her in math. Instead, Rory's dad gave her a lecture about lying and said that by not showing him the report card, it was the same as lying. Well, as far as Rory was concerned, taking her step sisters out to Pizza Pinazzo without her for their report card was worse than lying! Maybe her mom would take her out to her favorite restaurant, but it just wouldn't be the same.

"Ronald's Report Card Rally – WOW!"

After lunchtime at school, Ronald's teacher gave him an envelope for his dad and explained that it was a copy of his report card. Ronald wondered how his teacher knew that his parents were divorced; it had only just happened last month. Mrs. Woods explained that Ronald's parents told her about it in case he had any problems in school and needed someone to talk to. Ronald actually found it kind of fun to have two homes and two rooms. He did miss his dad when he was at his mom's and missed his mom when he was at his dad, but both his parents let him call the other one on the phone every night. He sometimes forgot to show his dad his school papers and his mom forgot to remind him – she seemed very preoccupied lately. Mrs. Woods explained that she would give him two copies of important school papers for Ronald to have one for each of his parents to help him remember to show his dad. The report card grades were a bit lower that the first quarter and Ronald knew he had to try harder. His mother had not been checking his homework when he was at his dad's. His dad set up a desk for studying and got him a new desk lamp that had his favorite sports teams written all over it. But it was hard to get used to doing his homework alone in his new room at his dad's house when he had always done it in the dining room while his mother cooked dinner. When he showed the report card to his dad, they talked about his grades and how he could improve them. Ronald was glad his dad was not angry and decided to take a chance and tell him about the homework problem. Ronald was worried that his dad would be upset because he spent a lot of money on the new lamp and Ronald overheard his parents talking about money problems. He was relieved when his father told him not to worry about the lamp and that he could do his homework in the kitchen while dad cooked. Well, dad didn't exactly do much cooking, but he did do his office work at the kitchen table while Ronald did his homework, after they had take out dinner. And Ronald liked having his dad next to him while he did his homework, even if he did not need help.

---

*Important points to remember about your child's report card

Report cards have been a tradition in schools for many years and will likely continue to be the traditional means of letting parents know the progress of their children's education. Children can be taught to understand how the grades are calculated throughout the quarter so they comprehend the importance of each test grade and completed homework assignment. Parents can best use the report card for a discussion about progress and goals for the future quarter along with specific daily plans to support the improvement goal. The best person to compare your child's grades to are their own expectations of themselves, their previous grades and their evaluation of their own best efforts.

Chapter Ten

Attendance: Avalanches or Awards

What is our child's school attendance policy?

Your child is expected to attend school every day on time for the full day. Special considerations for absences are given such as Dr. appointments, illness or death in the family. These are considered excused absences. Generally, absences for any other reason, or absences not reported to the school by the parent is considered an unexcused absence. Consideration is always given for special circumstances; however, make sure to check with your child's school district for their attendance policy. The student handbook distributed at registration or the first week of school will detail the attendance policy. A minimum number of days of attendance is required in order to be promoted to the next grade.

What is a tardy?

Arriving at school after the time the school day begins is considered late or tardy. This applies to Middle and High schools where students change classes throughout the day – arriving at a class late is considered tardy.

What is considered an excused absence vs. an unexcused absence?

Consult the student attendance policy in your child's school handbook for excused vs. unexcused absences. Illness, Dr. appointment and death in the family are excused absences. Most school districts do not consider a family vacation to be an excused absence; however, special considerations are given for certain circumstances. It is generally expected that the parent telephone the school to report an absence. Some schools have an automatic telephone system which phones parents when their child is absent.

What if my ex does not get our child to school on time?

On days your child spends the night at your home, it is the responsibility of that parent to be sure that the child arrives to school on time. The school will explain the importance of on time attendance and will address the problem with the parent if it becomes an ongoing problem.

What if our child misses the bus?

Getting children ready for school and out the door on time can be a challenge. If your child misses the school bus, it is the responsibility of the parent to make arrangements to get their child to school. If the bus company is at fault, sometimes the school district will send out another bus to pick your child up, however, young children should not be waiting unsupervised at a school bus stop for safety considerations. At the beginning of the school year, it is customary for the school bus driver to be late until the bus route is organized properly, thus parents need to be patient for several weeks. Your school district can provide you with a telephone number and procedure to report bus problems.

Which parent should stay home with our sick child?

Children get sick as a normal aspect of their growth and development throughout their school career. Joint custody parents should expect this occurrence and plan for it ahead of time. One parent might be in a better position than another to take off work unexpectedly, so this might not be an equitable plan. Back up arrangements can be planned for, such as a babysitter available at last minute notice, a relative, neighbor or sick child care through an employee's health insurance.

Which parent should be expected to leave work to pick up our sick child?

Your child getting sick at school and needing to be picked up in the middle of the school day is a contingency that joint custody parents should discuss before the beginning of the school year. A plan should be in place ahead of time to respond to this inconvenience without having your child feel responsible for illness. It might be best to discuss with your employer ahead of time the possibility of this occurrence as some companies are family friendly and are understanding of this situation. It is critical that this plan is in place ahead of time as schools are equipped to have a sick child rest for a short period of time, not the entire school day.

How can we be sure if our child is really sick enough to stay home from school?

Check with your child's doctor for guidelines as to when to keep your child home from school. There are three considerations here: your child's weakened immune system due to being sick, the overall general health of your child, and the possibility of spreading infection to others at school.

What if both parents disagree on whether our child should attend when sick?

Divorced parents as well as married parents often disagree on aspects of child-rearing and these disagreements need to be negotiated ahead of time. If your child suspects there are disagreements, one parent might be manipulated to allow a day off from school more often than the other parent. Some parents might keep their child home for an opportunity to spend more time together, a practice that can give your child a diminished sense of responsibility for the importance of school attendance.

Which parent is responsible for calling the school to report an absence?

Both parents should be aware of their child's absence from school since your child's health and school attendance is the responsibility of both joint custody parents. The school doesn't care which parent phones in the absence; however it is the responsibility of both parents to make sure that it is reported. Making a simple telephone call can be done by either parent, however, in order to avoid the call being forgotten, it may be best for the parent with whom the child is with to make the call. Schools require the absence to be reported by a parent so do not request your child to place this call.

Which parent will be telephoned to report an unexcused absence of our child?

Many school districts have installed a computer generated telephone program to phone the parent of the student's whose absences have not been reported to the school for the day. The number you provide to the school will be the telephone number phoned. If both joint custody parents wish to be phoned, ask your child's school if two numbers can be provided.

What if we are contacted by the school social worker for too many absences?

School districts generally employ a school social worker to help with school problems such as attendance issues. Since school attendance is mandatory for children between the ages of six and sixteen in this country, legal action against parents can be employed if it is suspected that parents are not ensuring their child's regular school attendance. This problem is referred to as truancy. Joint custody parents having conflicts with school attendance for their child may be able to receive assistance from the school social worker.

What is our child's responsibility regarding school attendance?

Your child is responsible to get ready on time and be prepared to attend school each day. Your child is also responsible to talk to both parents about any emotional issues or school problems which cause him/her to want to avoid school. Your child is responsible to be truthful when sick and not try to avoid school by pretending to be sick.

How can we help our child learn responsibility for his/her school attendance?

Both joint custody parents can help their child become responsible for their school attendance by carefully evaluating any illness which might cause your child to need to remain absent and by promoting the importance of daily school attendance. Children should not be requested to stay home to baby-sit a sibling.

"Andy's Attendance Avalanche – Oops!"

"Guess what!" excitedly proclaimed Andy's dad. "Your cousins are coming in from out of town and we are going to go to the zoo, the amusement park, the movies, the game room, bowling and the batting cages for the entire week!!" "When?" asked Andy, thinking of the great fun he had with his cousins last summer. "In two weeks, at the beginning of the month, during their school holiday". Since his cousins lived out of town, their school vacation was different than Andy's and Andy knew he had school that week. How important could second grade be anyway, thought Andy, maybe he could take the week off. After all, that was the week he was with his dad. Since his parents had gotten a divorce, he lived with his dad one week and his mom the next. Andy had a calendar at both parents home, both on the refrigerator to help him remember where he was supposed to be each week. Andy reminded his dad that he had school and mentioned that his mother would not approve of him taking off from school. His dad was prepared for that and smiled slyly: "Let's keep it our little secret". Andy really wanted to spend time with his cousins and couldn't imagine why a week off from second grade would matter. His best friend, Joseph, took a week off when he was sick with the flu. Joseph's cousins lived nearly and he got to see them almost every weekend so it was only fair that Andy got to take a week off to be with his cousins! What's fair is fair!! But, he also remembered the pact he had with his mom – no secrets. Andy also knew he was having field day at school that week and had been looking forward to it all school year. But fun with his cousins was more fun than anything in the world, maybe even in the universe and Andy couldn't wait to show them his new video games!! The next week at his mom's house, Andy struggled to keep his special secret but he was so excited and nervous at the same time that his mother noticed something was different. When she finally asked him what wrong, he burst out in tears was and told her about the secret pact he made with his dad and the plan to take off from school and his excitement to see his cousins. His mother held him in her arms, told him everything was going to be alright but that he could not take off from school. Later that night when he was supposed to be sleeping, Andy overheard his mother calling his father and yelling at him. Andy also heard her calling him names that he knew were not allowed and threatened something to do with court. He didn't exactly know what court had to do with it but knew that it was not a good thing by the tone of her voice. He was very worried that his dad would be angry with him for not keeping the secret and worried the entire week about seeing his dad. When he finally did see his dad, Andy was told that his cousins were still visiting but that he would have to go to school each day or his mom would have his dad arrested! He also told him that it was his mom's fault that he could not have fun with his cousins and that she just wanted to keep Andy from having a life with his dad and his relatives. Andy was no longer looking forward to seeing his cousins, nor was he looking forward to field day at school. He wished he could be Joseph, his best friend whose parents were not divorced.

"Ariel's Attendance Award – WOW!"

Ariel got a "C" in math for her last quarter of fifth grade, which was like an "A" for someone else, thought Ariel. She had been failing math most of the year, but worked so hard, with her mother, her father and her tutor, as well as after school help with her teacher. Her three best friends got all "A's", except an occasional "B" in all their subjects, while Ariel struggled to not get "D's" and "F's". She had a learning disability which made it difficult for her to read and calculate numbers, but at least now she was in a regular class, even if it was hard for her. Her parents, who were divorced, agreed with each other when they constantly reminded her that she was an "A+" person, when it came to being kind, helpful and generous to others. Now that the school year was finally over and the last awards assembly was almost over, Ariel looked forward to summer break. She tried not to feel sad as her friends were receiving awards for best in science, best in math, best speller, etc. The assembly went on and on and Ariel felt a bit embarrassed that her parents were there when she hadn't excelled in anything. Back to daydreaming about her summer break - the first month was to be spent with her dad, with two weeks at home and two weeks traveling to see her grandparents across the other side of the country. The second month was with her mom where she would attend a horseback riding camp that her parents both saved for all year. The principal was calling Ariel's name on the loudspeaker, announcing an award, and Ariel almost didn't even hear her until her friends pushed her and loudly whispered to for her to go up on stage. Everyone was clapping loudly, maybe even louder than for the other awards. The principal gave Ariel a plaque for "Perfect Attendance" for kindergarten through fifth grade – her entire school career – AND – Ariel was the only one!!!!!!!!!!!!!!!!!!! The principal, Ms. Montgomery, made a speech about the importance of school attendance and invited her parents up to the stage to share in the award. Ariel knew they both deserved it since she was sure they had a secret agreement to never let her stay absent from school. When she was struggling with her schoolwork and didn't want to go, they both always recited the same speech about the importance of school attendance. Now that Ms. Montgomery was making the same speech, it made more sense. Ariel was sure that she felt more proud than her friends did for their award, but knew that her parents felt even prouder.

---

*Important points to remember about your child's attendance

School attendance is an opportunity for parents to instill responsibility in their children, which will set the stage for responsibility for their future work career. Both joint custody parents share in this responsibility, regardless of their differing views in childrearing. Your child's school schedule should be considered when planning family visits and activities, avoiding giving your child the message that school attendance is optional. Both parents will need to work hard to consistently instill this value in their children.

Part II

Significant
School Events
for Your Child

Chapter Eleven

School Uniforms and School Clothing: Underworld or Upright

How many full school uniforms does our child need?
The number of school uniforms needed will vary as to how often your child spends the evening before the school day at your home and how often you do laundry. Five complete uniforms per child if your child spends school nights at one home only should be enough. More in total may be needed for convenience if your child sleeps at both parents homes during the school week.

How often do the school uniforms need to be replaced?
School uniforms should be replaced when your child wears them out or outgrows them. At times, a healthy growing child may out grow uniforms before the school year is over, necessitating the purchase of a larger size.

Which parent should pay for the uniforms?
The cost of the school uniforms should be discussed and negotiated before the start of the school year so that there is no delay in providing your child with the required uniforms. This might be considered into the cost of school supplies or clothing allowance when negotiating other financial aspects of your joint custody arrangement.

How many uniforms should be kept at each household?
You should consider keeping at least one uniform per school night that your child sleeps at your home and an extra just in case of last minute emergencies.

Which parent should be responsible for washing the school uniforms?

Both parents should be responsible for washing the school uniforms when your child is at your home. Remember that the uniform belongs to your child, not you or your ex, so the uniforms may be switched between two different homes during the week.

What if the uniforms get lost between households?

An extra uniform at each joint custody parent's home will avoid further problems until your child develops more responsibility for their uniforms.

How much responsibility should our child be expected to take for his/her school uniforms?

Your child can learn how to select, pack, wash, and repair their uniform as they get older. Begin teaching them responsibility at an early age until they have mastered caring for their own school uniforms. The age you teach your child will depend upon your personal parenting style and your child's abilities. Remember that learning responsibility enhances self worth and confidence.

How can we help our child learn to take responsibility for uniforms?

You can have your child help shop for school uniforms even if you know their size, help with the washing and packing if bringing uniforms between two homes.

How can we find out the school's dress code?

Some schools have a required uniform, while others have a uniform dress code which specifies the style and color of shirt and pants to be worn. Some schools allow a wide range of attire with special rules detailed in the dress code policy. A detailed dress code is included in the student handbook provided at the beginning of the school year to each student and their families. Ask for two copies, which both joint custody parents should sign indicating their awareness of the school dress code as well as all other rules. Note that special exceptions to the dress code are made for families with religious or other reasons – talk with your child's school for more information about these exceptions.

What if my ex does not enforce the school dress code?

Enforcement of the school dress code is the responsibility of both joint custody parents and their children. Consequences for not following the school dress code are clearly spelled out in the student code of conduct, however not necessarily consistently enforced. Your child will eventually receive a consequence for violating dress code, which will be between your child and the school to comply with.

How can we help our child feel positive about uniforms?

If all the children at the school are wearing uniforms, there is less distraction regarding clothing and often a higher degree of school pride and school spirit. If you feel that your child looks great and convey such, then your child will most likely adapt your opinion. Unless of course, they are teenagers and will likely find a style of their own even with their school uniform – be amazed at their creativity!

"Ursula's School Uniform Underworld – Oops!"

Ursula's dad had just been awarded joint custody and an equal living arrangement by the courts and her mom was crying. Ursula did not know what that meant but understood that she would be spending half the week at her dad's house – Sunday through Wednesday. Her older brother and sister would also be spending the same time there with her and she would be sharing a room with her older sister, just like at her mom's house. As long as she went where they went, Ursula knew she didn't have to keep track of the days, since she was only in kindergarten and just beginning to learn the days of the week. And as long as her sister was with her in the mornings, she could help Ursula get dressed for school. So why was her mother crying? Her older brother told her that her mom was just worried about missing them but that it would be alright, and out of his pocket came a piece of gum! Ursula's brother and sister took such good care of her, they kept telling her that everything would be alright whenever her parents fought loudly and when they finally divorced. She felt safe with them whenever her mom would be crying which was a lot lately. At her dad's house, Ursula shared the same room with her sister that she used to on weekends, but now dad would be taking her to school on Monday, Tuesday and Wednesday mornings. At least she went to the same school as her sister, so she would not be alone. Everything was going to be alright. Except it was not! The first Monday morning she went to school from her dad's she did not have her uniform with her. She overheard her dad calling her mom early in the morning saying it was her mother's responsibility to pack the uniform. Her dad told her that this was her mom's fault and asked Ursula to speak directly to her mom and ask her to bring her uniform to her. Why did she have to get in the middle of a fight between her mom and dad? When Ursula asked her mom to bring her uniform to her dad's house, her mother said that she would drop off the uniform at school instead, but that it was her dads' responsibility to purchase her school uniforms for his house if she were going to be spending school nights there. She sounded angry at Ursula and Ursula wondered again if the divorce were her fault. Her older sister kept telling her that it was not her fault even though all the fights she overheard were about her and her brother and sister. She had a stomach ache again and did not want to go to school but her sister said she would feel better later. When her dad dropped all three of them off at school, her sister took her to the front office just in time to see her mother dropping off the uniform and telling the office secretary that Ursula's dad was too irresponsible as a father to get her school uniforms. She was so embarrassed she wanted to turn right around and leave. Her mom hugged her and told her she loved her and reminded Ursula that mom never would forget her uniform. Ursula thought that she should feel better but she started to wonder about her uniform for the next day, since she knew she was spending the night at her dad's again. Her sister told her that they would wash her uniform and it would all work out fine .But Ursula' stomach was starting to hurt again when her kindergarten class began the day with circle time and the day of the week…Monday…the uniform disaster day!

"Umberto's School Uniform Upright – WOW!

Umberto's mom took great pride in setting out his clothes for school the night before. She washed and even ironed his school clothes which were khaki pants and a white collared shirt. She said he looked so "spiffy", and Umberto thought that was a funny word and laughed each time she said it. Once a week, he slept at his dad's house during the school week, on Wednesday evenings and every other weekend, an arrangement which he quickly got accustomed to since his parents divorced two years ago. His mom always sent his school clothes for Thursday mornings when she would pack his clothing for the weekend. She even sent over an extra set of school clothes at the beginning of the school year to keep at his dad's house "just in case". Umberto wasn't sure what just in case was, but he was glad it had not happened. He knew his mom was always thinking ahead of time with having extra school supplies at home and lots of extra laundry detergent she said she picked up on sale. Umberto's mom also said that he would have to begin to learn to take care of his clothes – washing them and packing them for his dad's each week. Umberto wasn't sure if his dad's washing machine was working – there were lots of dirty clothes lying around all the time in his dad's room. Actually, his dad had a lot of things out of order at his house and was always saying that he had to clean it up one of these days. Once when Umberto offered to help him, they wound up playing a video game instead. Umberto was actually glad that his mom sent him with clothes, since he really had no place at his dad's house to keep extra clothes. He slept on a pullout sofa couch which was actually a lot of fun. His dad made sure the TV and lights were off so Umberto could get a good night sleep and Umberto slept with his special superhero blanket his mom sent with him each week. He knew she washed it between visits because it always smelled like her laundry detergent when he took it out of his bag. Sometimes if he forgot to wash his face in the morning and brush his teeth, his dad forgot to remind him and twice, they both overslept and Umberto got to school late. That did not happened again when his mom sent him with a cool alarm clock of his own, also with superheroes on it! Umberto was learning to wake himself up for school and remembering to wash his face and brush his teeth almost all the time now. One morning when he was all ready for school he asked his father what "spiffy" meant. His dad told him that it meant he was very handsome and Umberto smiled widely. He secretly thought he looked spiffy in his school uniform too!

*Important points to remember about your child's school uniforms

Your child's school uniform is an extension of their feelings about school and themselves. Make sure to be sensitive to your child's feeling by making clear plans ahead of time with your ex as to how to handle the uniform issue. If a mistake is made, it is worth your child's self esteem for you to go the extra mile and help out. Do not use your child's school uniform to take out your anger or frustration at your ex spouse.

Chapter Twelve

Picture Day: Dilemmas or Dreams

What is picture day?

Picture Day is a time honored tradition in schools where a photographer is hired to take individual and class pictures of students at school.

Why is picture day important?

Picture Day is important because it provides your child with a sense of identity and belonging, increasing self esteem and helping them to feel part of their class and their school.

How can we find out when picture day is scheduled?

Schools send home notices approximately three weeks in advance of picture day with an order form from the individual private photography company. The date of picture day is often printed in the school newsletter, on the school's website, and in community newspapers.

What should our child wear for picture day?

Picture day forms usually advise which colors would look best with the backgrounds available. Sometimes there is a variety of backgrounds to choose from. Your child should wear something that is simple, neat and clean. It is very important that your child wear clothing that (s)he feels good in. The class picture may show the entire outfit if your child is in the front row. The individual picture is usually taken just above the waist.

Should I let my ex know when order forms for pictures are sent home?

Definitely! If possible, arrange to have a duplicate order form which you can provide for your ex for review. Encourage him/her to select a package with relatives in mind. Only one order form should be given to the school, however since the bookkeeping between the school and the photographer is complicated. Combine both orders and send the combined order to your child' school by the due date.

Which parent should pay for the pictures?

Each parent should pay for their own ordered package of pictures. Collect the money from your ex and send only one check or money order in to the school with the order form. It may be difficult for you to deal with your ex regarding money issues, however, do not let this get in the way of your child's positive picture day experience.

What if our child says (s)he does not care about pictures?

Children say they that they do not care about many things when they really do care. Even if your child does not care at the moment, feelings may change when classmates are handing in their order forms and on the actual day of pictures. His/her classmates will be arriving at school wearing their favorite clothes, the class will be called down to the auditorium to line up and wait for their picture, individually and with the class, and a big fuss will be made in school when the pictures arrive. Your child may feel left out at these times if (s)he did not participate.

How many pictures should I order?

Think about who you and your child would like to have a picture of him/her. Generally, grandparents and close relatives like to have a picture to display. Inexpensive frames are made in standard 4x6, 5x7, and 8x10. Small wallet sized pictures are good to carry and use in craft projects such as Christmas ornaments, Valentine's Day cards and other homemade gifts. Older children and teens like to exchange wallet sized pictures with their friends. Having a friend carry or display your child's picture is a big ego boost!

Can I just copy the original at a photo center?

Professional school pictures taken by a photographer have an imprint on the back alerting photo shops that it is illegal to photocopy them. That is because it cuts into their business. Of course you can

60

sneak a copy at a do it yourself machine, however, this is a bad example for your child. The extra expense is worth the lesson in honesty and the extra self esteem boost for your child when you pre-order a package from the photographer. Extra copies are available for order at a premium price if you really love the way the picture came out. Retakes are sometimes done at the studio, but only for closed eyes or photographer error.

Who should I give my child's picture to?

Make a list of relatives and close friends who would appreciate a picture of your child and proudly display it or carry in their wallet. The more people who express pride in your child, the bigger opportunity for enhanced self esteem. This is especially important for children whose parents are divorced.

What is our child's responsibility regarding school pictures?

Your child is responsible for bringing home all notices and order forms about picture day in a timely manner. Your child is responsible to return the order form and payment to the teacher. Your child should help select who to give pictures to, what to wear on picture day and smile proudly for the picture.

How can we help picture day to be a positive experience for our child?

You can act excited about having school pictures taken of your child, even share stories about your youthful experiences with school pictures. You can discuss who will be given pictures and how happy they will be to receive them. You can make certain to return the picture day form to your child's school on time. You can help select the best outfit, make sure your child is clean with hair washed and combed, and remind your child to smile. When pictures arrive home, be sure to act excited again, avoiding negative comments about a hair out of place or a crooked smile. Pay careful attention to avoiding complaints about the expense – your child's simple thinking may interpret that as (s)he is not worth much. Think of creative uses for extra pictures such as framed gifts for relatives for holidays, birthdays, Mother's Day, Father's Day, Grandparent's Day and Valentine's Day. Your child will beam with pride when giving a framed picture of him/herself to a loved one and receiving great joy and gratitude for such a wonderful gift! Picture Day can provide many benefits in raising and maintaining self esteem for all children, especially for children from divorced families.

Derrick's Picture Day Dilemma

Derrick was so excited when the teacher handed out the forms for picture day in his first grade class. He couldn't wait to have his photo taken by the school photographer and get his pictures back later that month in class. His two older cousins on his dad's side always proudly gave their grandmother their school pictures each year. She made such a big fuss about how handsome they looked and hung up the pictures on her special picture wall in the living room for everyone to see as soon as they came through the door of her home. This year Derrick would surprise her with a picture of himself! He already picked out the blue shirt he would wear which would look really cool just like his cousins. There were three packages of pictures to choose from, Derrick hoped his mom would pick the biggest one and he hoped it was not too expensive. Derrick knew his mom did not have a lot of money since she and his dad got a divorce last year. She made a point of mentioning it whenever Derrick said he wanted something. But he wanted this picture more than he wanted the newest Viper video game and even more than he wanted to go to Adventure Theme Land, the coolest new theme park in their town.

Derrick often forgot to tell his mom when he brought home important papers from school, but not his time. He could barely wait until she signed him out of aftercare before he unzipped his backpack and showed his mom the picture order form! At least he tried to show it to her, but his mom said not now, she was already running late to get back home and had a terrible headache already. Derrick's mom had a lot of terrible headaches since the divorce and Derrick knew to be really quiet whenever that happened. He waited until later that night at bedtime to talk with her about the school pictures. Derrick made sure he ate all his dinner, did all his homework, brushed his teeth and even remembered to hang up his towel after his bath. Maybe that would put his mom in a good mood – she always got so angry when he forgot to hang up his towel, which was most of the time. Derrick could barely contain himself from waiting any longer and burst out telling her about school picture day and the largest picture package and how he would wear his blue shirt, but it all came out so fast, his mom said: "stop, wait, lets worry about that tomorrow – I have to do the laundry and the dishes and pay the bills tonight and I can barely stay awake another minute!" Derrick tried hard not to show his disappointment but he wondered why his mom was tired all the time since the divorce. He would just wait and ask her tomorrow.

But he forgot to ask her tomorrow and when he asked her the next day, she was tired again and had another terrible headache. Derrick had another plan. He would ask his father when he saw him over the weekend. His father seemed to have a lot of money each weekend and didn't mind spending it on Derrick. He bought Derrick almost anything he asked for – well almost anything. He wouldn't buy him a pretty necklace he saw for his mother last month for her birthday – Derrick's dad said he should just make her a card instead. Derrick would have made her a card but he didn't know how to so he gave her a picture he made in school. His mother smiled and said it was the nicest picture and hung it up on the fridge. Derrick notices that she still smiles whenever she looks at it.

Derrick forgot to ask his father about picture day and when he got back to school his teacher said that tomorrow was the last day to hand in the picture order form. He would certainly remember to ask his mother tonight and she would of course order a picture since he knew she loved him very much. Finally, Derrick got to tell his mom about picture day and how he wanted to wear his blue shirt and order enough pictures for everyone in his whole family. He didn't tell her about how he wanted one especially for his grandmother's wall. He knew his mother was angry at his grandmother but didn't know why. Maybe it was because she was angry at his dad and his grandmother was his dad's mother. It was all too confusing for him anyway. His mother said she would look at the form and think about it. He was sure she would order a picture!

The next morning, Derrick could hardly wait to ask his mother about the picture order form. He often forgot his lunch, his jacket or even his homework but he certainly remembered the picture order form. How could he forget, today was the last day to hand it in. He was very disappointed and wanted to cry when his mother said that the school pictures were too expensive and she would take her own picture of him. He knew he needed to try to understand, that he could not have everything he wanted but he wanted the school picture so much – couldn't he just have that and nothing else? Derrick tried to tell his mother that a picture she took was not the same as a school picture, but his mother thought he was being silly and even selfish. She thought it would make him feel better if she changed the subject and let him have a doughnut for breakfast, but he wasn't that hungry. Derrick didn't even want to go to school that day, but he knew he had to.

Derrick's teacher reminded the class that only two students didn't hand in their picture order form and he wanted to cry. At least he was not the only one, but that didn't make him feel any better. On picture day, Derrick wore his blue shirt, hoping maybe a miracle would happen and his picture would be taken with the rest of his class. They all were escorted to the auditorium and waited on line. All the students were given a brand new small black comb. Did this mean he might have his picture taken? Derrick was deflated when his name in the alphabet was passed over. It was hard for him to smile when his picture was finally taken with the entire class for the class picture. Maybe he could cut his face out of the school picture and give that to his grandmother. Maybe not, it would look too dorky next to his cousins' big class pictures.

Dahlia's Picture Dream

Dahlia had the prettiest smile in the world! At least that was what her dad said, but by the time she was twelve last month, she was old enough to know that her dad could not have seen the smiles of every-one in the world! Still, her dad always insisted that hers was the prettiest and it only made Dahlia want to smile even more, even when her dad was not around. Secretly, she wondered if others thought she had a pretty smile and often she was complimented on her beautiful smile. If her dad thought it she was pretty, maybe some boys would think so to, since after all, her dad was a boy! She only just admitted to her best friend, Susan, that she liked boys and only after Susan told her first.

When the picture order form was handed out in Dahlia's sixth grade homeroom class, she shoved it in her backpack. Both her parents had so many pictures of her all over both their homes already. Dahlia's parents had been divorced since she was six, and she lived with her mother most of the time. If you were ever at her father's home, you would think she lived there by the dozens of photos of Dahlia around his entire house!

Dahlia began her homework as soon as she got home that day and waited for her mother to return home from work. This was the first year she was permitted to stay home alone after school but it was only for two hours. When Dahlia's mother arrived home, she quickly put dinner in the oven and checked her daughter's homework. She was so glad to see that it was almost finished and Dahlia understood the entire math assignment. Last week she thought she might have to hire a tutor and did not know where she would find the money. What was that stuffed in the bottom of the backpack? The picture order form was all crushed, but Dahlia's mother unfolded it and read through it carefully. Next month was Dahlia's father's birthday and she had an idea. She ordered a set of school photographs for herself, her relatives, her ex and his relatives too. Dahlia might like to give a framed photo of herself to her father for his birthday and she knew how much he loved pictures of Dahlia. There were some really neat frames at the local dollar store that Dahlia could buy herself.

Later that month, Dahlia gave her dad a birthday present that she paid for herself with her own allowance! (At least the money for the frame came from her allowance) Her father was so surprised, or at least he acted like he was and said it was the best present he could have received from his beautiful daughter with the prettiest smile in the world. Dahlia made sure she smiled her most beautiful smile when her school picture was taken since her mother told her the secret plan for her father's birthday gift. Her father was even more surprised when she showed up with six individually wrapped presents for all of her relatives gathered at her grandmother's house for the Christmas holiday. There was one a bit bigger than the rest for his mother, Dahlia's grandmother, who doted on her even more than her father did. When it was time to unwrap the gifts, Dahlia made an announcement. She was proud to tell her aunts, uncles and cousins that this was the first year that she purchased all of the gifts with her own money that she saved from her allowance! (Even though her mother paid for the pictures, Dahlia paid for the frames and her mom told her that really meant that she paid for the gifts herself.) Dahlia missed her mother a little on Christmas Day that year since it was her father's turn to have her with his family. She worried that her mother would be sad all alone, but Dahlia's mother assured her that she had great plans with her best friend and would call Dahlia in the evening. Her mom felt so happy when Dahlia proudly told her the reactions of her grandmother and aunts when she gave them the framed photographs for Christmas. Even though Dahlia was not with her, she looked at the identical school photograph she had hung up on the wall of her living room and felt so lucky to have a daughter with the most beautiful smile in the entire world.

---

*Important points to remember about your child's picture day

Both Derrick and Dahlia's mothers loved their children very much. Derrick's mother was so consumed by her bitterness towards her ex, that she was blocked from considering or even noticing how important school pictures were to her son. Dahlia's mother also had negative feelings about her ex and the divorce, however she was able to set those feelings aside in order to consider how she could make school pictures a meaningful event for her daughter. Think about ways that you can make your child's school picture day a positive experience and ways you can help avoid negative memories or possibly trauma. You can do this by putting your child's normal need for ongoing positive affirmation before your need to express your sadness, anger and bitterness towards your ex. Your child will benefit and you will be immeasurably happier and feel more confident as a parent!

Chapter Thirteen

Field Trips: Fiascos or Fantasies

What is the purpose of school field trips?
School field trips are designed to enhance the material taught in the classroom, to cultivate a variety of interests and expose your children to various cultural opportunities. It is often a bonding experience for the class, the club or the grade levels in that classmates have a lot of fun together outside of school.

How is the cost of a field trip computed?
Schools receive a discounted fee for large group admissions, sometimes covered by governmental or private grants. The cost of chaperones and teacher's admission fees and bus transportation is included as well as meals if provided.

Which parent should pay for field trips?
Joint custody parents may wish to consult with your child's teacher at the beginning of the school year to learn what types of field trips are planned, and the expense. Depending upon the grade level, there are sometimes overnight field trips offered which can run into the hundreds of dollars. A discussion about the payment of field trip expenses should occur before the permission slips are sent home in order to avoid your child getting caught in the middle of an adult decision.

Is it important for our child to participate in every field trip?
Not every student in the class will be attending every field trip, but often the students left behind are those who were removed for reasons of behavior problems. The single day field trips generally are attended by most students and the class looks forward to these trips away from school.

What if we can not afford the field trips?

Your child's school may have a special fund to cover the expenses of those deserving students who are unable to afford the cost of the field trip. Put your embarrassment aside and ask your child's teacher. Grandparents, aunts and uncles are often happy to assist with these extra perks – ask if they have expressed an interest in helping.

Can I chaperone a field trip?

School field trips will often request parents to volunteer to chaperone. Some school districts are now requiring criminal background checks on parents volunteering or chaperoning field trips for the protection of all of the students. This process takes time so check into this early in the school year. .

Do I have to pay if I chaperone?

School field trips generally cover the cost of a certain number of chaperones. If more parents volunteer, they are often permitted to attend if they pay there own fees.

What are the benefits of my volunteering to chaperone field trips?

You will have an opportunity to observe your child's teacher, your child's classmates, your own child, and the interaction of the class. You will meet other parents of your child's classmates and you may have a great time!

Is it really worth my taking a day off from work for a field trip?

One day off a school year to chaperone your child's school field trip will be invaluable for you in seeing firsthand and understanding the nuances that your child cannot explain to you about their teacher and classmates.

What if our child does not want me to chaperone?

Perhaps your child feels that your presence will spoil their fun time with their friends. Many children are proud to have their parent chaperone. If your child asks you, jump at the chance!

How can we find out ahead of time which field trips will be sched-uled?

Check with your child's teacher at the beginning of the school year to learn which field trips are being planned for that school year.

What is the responsibility of a parent chaperone on a field trip?

The parent chaperone on a school field trip will be responsible for helping the teacher to monitor the students in the class. Your child's teacher might assign a small group of students for you to be responsible for throughout the trip. As the teacher's assistant, your child's teacher will inform you of the various responsibilities as the trip ensues, such as handing out lunches, helping to quiet the children, assisting the line to move forward and ensuring safety procedures are adhered to are some examples.

How much money does our child need to take for souvenirs, meal and snacks?

The field trip form will indicate whether or not meals are included and whether extra spending money is needed. Souvenirs tend to be expensive at many of these locations so it is advisable to negotiate with your child how much money will be allotted for such. This is a good opportunity for your child to be permitted to spend money they have been saving on their own.

Which parent should provide spending money?

The joint custody parents should discuss and decide this ahead of time so that your child is properly prepared on the day of the field trip. Both parents may wish to contribute to your child's special day.

Should we provide limits as to what our child can purchase?

The field trip gift shop may be your child's first opportunity to spend money without a parent or guardian present to limit or advise. Discuss limits with your child ahead of time.

Is our child responsible enough to carry spending money?

This is a good opportunity to begin small with teaching your child the responsibility of carrying money and not losing it. If there is a need for your child to have a larger amount of money than you feel they are responsible for, consider requesting your child's teacher or one of the parent chaperones to carry their money for them.

What if our child has a medical condition or takes medication?

Alert your child's teacher to any medical conditions in addition to indicating so on the field trip permission form. The school's medication policy applies on field trips with very particular specification to be followed. If you would be more comfortable monitoring your child's medical condition during a school field trip, consider volunteering as a chaperone.

How do we handle overnight field trips?

Not all students attend overnight field trips due to the expense involved and sometimes the discomfort of their family. Those that do attend generally save up for much of the school year with contributions from relatives. The material being studied in your child's grade level will determine the location of the overnight field trip. Some are well organized by the site such as a nature camp or space camp. Others are organized by qualified tour companies such as trips to historical sites. Overnight field trips need parent chaperones as well so if your child is asking to go, and you are not sure of your own comfort level, consider volunteering to chaperone. It is a wonderful opportunity for your child to develop independence and confidence.

What if both parents disagree on whether or not our child should attend?

Joint custody divorced parents disagree on many things; however, for the best interest of your child, a compromise needs to be reached early on so as not to put your child in the middle of your disagreement. Gather the facts from your child's teacher or Guidance Counselor in order to be better informed of what the field trip entails. Discuss your child's particular needs and abilities with his/her pediatrician or therapist to come to an agreement.

What about safety on school field trips?

Your child's school principal or school district will not approve of a school field trip not deemed safe. Allowing your child to attend a school field trip is voluntary, and you may choose to have your child skip the field trip if you are not personally comfortable with the safety measures in place. There might be alternatives worth pursuing such as driving your child in your own vehicle instead of having them take the chartered or school bus.

What is our child's responsibility on school field trips?
Your child is responsible to bring home the field trip permission form and discuss the field trip with both parents, demonstrate good manners and their best behavior while on the field trip. Your child is also responsible to respect your decision about participation in field trips and respect your limits regarding spending money.

How can we help our child be responsible on school field trips?
It would be best for both joint custody parents to discuss expectations of rules and manners with your child before each field trip.

"Fran's Field Trip Fiasco – Oops!"

Fran was so excited about the class trip being planned to the zoo since she had wanted to be a veterinarian ever since she knew what that was. Her teachers kept telling her to keep her grades up and Fran earned all A's and B's right through middle school. The only time she got a C and a D was three years ago right before her parents finally got a divorce and they fought all the time. They still fought all the time, even though they no longer lived together and Fran often wondered why. She overheard arguments about money and court, but her Guidance Counselor told her that those were adult problems that she needed to let her parents worry about. The entire eighth grade class of two hundred students was going on this field trip, at least those who were not suspended and got their field trip form and money in by this Friday. Fran's dad told her to ask her mom and her mom told her to ask her dad for the money. She wished she had her own money and did not need to bring up the topic of money to either her mom or her dad because that always ended up in an explanation about how the other parent was not being responsible about money and something to do with court and lawyers. Why did lawyers need to get involved in an eighth grade field trip to the zoo, Fran wondered. She wanted to talk to her friend Maria's mother about the problem, but Fran got in trouble with both of her parents the last time she did that. Maria's mother thought she was helping out by giving her the money for the field trip to the museum last year, but Fran's mother got angry and said that her dad got away with it again, as always. Fran's mom was bound and determined to make sure that her dad paid for this field trip and expected Fran to make sure that he did. But her dad said he gives her mother enough money in child support to pay for the whole school to go on a field trip and he was not giving her mother any more money. Fran tried to explain about the money being for her, his daughter, and her dreams of being a veterinarian and how hard she worked for her grades. The more Fran tried to explain this to him, the more he kept saying how uncaring and greedy her mom was to spend all the child support payments on manicures and expensive clothes for herself. By Thursday, Fran was out of ideas and began to feel defeated. She felt so guilty about telling her friend Maria that she hated both her parents. She knew she was supposed to love them both equally, but Fran knew that they were equally more angry with each other than they ever loved her and began to wonder why she worked so hard for her good grades all these years. Who cared about the stupid zoo and those smelly animals anyway!

"Freddy's Field Trip Fantasy – WOW!"

Freddy's dad was not sure what to expect as a chaperone for Freddy's second grade class for their field trip to the aquarium, but he had never seen Freddy as excited as he was this morning. It was Freddy's mom, his ex-wife who suggested that he volunteer to chaperone when the field trip permission form came home. Even though they had been divorced for a full year, she always knew what Freddy needed from his dad, even when his dad had no idea what to do. Seeing the look of excitement on his son's face reminded him that he was grateful that his ex-wife did not have animosity toward him for his decision to divorce her. At least she did not show it, when it concerned Freddy. Before he could even get out of his car, Freddy was dragging him excitedly over to the bus to meet his teacher and his best friend, Eddie. Freddy's dad had been hearing about Eddie for the entire school year, but seeing Freddy and Eddie together finally conveyed him to how important this friendship was to his son. Eddie's mom smiled warmly at him and said how glad she was to have him chaperoning the field trip. As the boys made plans to sit together on the big tour bus, Eddie's mom continued to talk to Freddy's dad. She seemed genuinely glad to meet him and shared that Freddy talks about his dad: "all the time." Freddy had asked his dad if Eddie could join them at times when they go to the movies or the park, but Freddy's dad thought that he was supposed to spend time alone with his son during their weekend visits. Maybe he would ask Eddie's mom if Freddy could come along one time – seeing how happy the boys were together finally reminded him of his own childhood friends.

The group of children Freddy's dad was responsible to monitor were all shapes and sizes, even though they were the same age. They all had their own personalities, which Freddy's dad came to know and enjoy during the bus ride, the tour of the aquarium and during lunchtime. On the bus ride back to school, Freddy's dad sat with Mrs. Price, the teacher. She told him about some of Freddy's strengths such as befriending shy students new to the school. His dad did not know that Freddy was the student selected to orient new students to his class because he was so friendly and accepting of all. Mrs. Price actually complimented Freddy's dad on doing such a fine job of raising him! As he looked back to see his son sleeping on the bus, along with almost every other eight year old, they all looked like angels. Freddy's dad finally understood why his ex-wife pushed him into being a field trip chaperone, and knew that he would do this every year from now on.

*Important points to remember about your child's school field trips

The benefits of chaperoning your child's school field trip are numerous. Observing a group of children the same age as your own, observing your own child interacting with his or her classmates and friends, meeting your child's friends and classmates, their parents, observing and getting to know your child's teacher, and bonding in a shared fun experience with your child and his or her class are some of the unique opportunities you will experience when chaperoning your child's field trip. It is worth a yearly planned day off from work to have this memory which you and your child will share for a lifetime!

Chapter Fourteen

Fund Raising: Frenzy or Fun

What is the purpose of fund raisers in school?

Fund Raisers at school are to promote school unity, school spirit, supplement the school budget, teach leadership skills, responsibility, and community service.

Does every child have to participate in school fund raisers?

Each child is encouraged to participate in school fund raisers which generally is introduced at a school wide assembly and followed up with a contest between the classes.

Why are the products so expensive?

The products your child will be selling such as chocolate or wrapping paper is expensive since a large portion of the profits benefit the school.

Is it necessary to ask my coworkers to participate?

You may ask anyone you are comfortable with to support your child's school fund raiser. Often coworkers support each other's children's fund raisers as way of supporting the parenting experience.

Should both parents participate in the fund raisers?

It is important to your child that both parents as well as close relatives support their fund raising efforts by making at least one single purchase, even if it is the least expensive item.

Which parent should keep the collected funds at their home?

The collected funds and documented paperwork should be kept in one home in order to maintain organization. The home which the child spends most of his/her school week would be best, however, if an equal amount of time is spent at each home, it would be best to allow your child to decide the best place to maintain the funds and records.

What if our child loses the money collected?

Being responsible about money is an important lesson for your child to learn. If (s)he still has not mastered this task, both parents will need to help teach this responsibility. Having your child do work chores to earn back the lost money would assist in becoming more responsible with money. It would be best if this is done in a supportive and not punitive way.

What is our child's responsibility regarding school fund raisers?

Your child is responsible to bring home all fundraising forms and directions, discuss with both parents, work with parents to develop a plan and maintain all records and collected money responsibly.

How can we use school fund raisers to help our child learn responsibility?

School fund raisers are perfect to help teach your child money management, organization skills, social skills and encourage confidence building.

What if both parents disagree on whether our child should participate?

Just as any school issue that joint custody parents disagree on, this needs to be discussed out of earshot of your child and the agreed upon compromise presented to your child as a united front.

How can we help make a fund raiser a positive opportunity for our child?

By presenting a positive attitude, encouraging your child to participate, providing ideas and directions for fund raising, as well as accompanying your child in his/her efforts, you will be helping to make the school fund raiser a positive experience for your child. You may wish to consider further assisting their efforts by purchasing gifts from the fundraiser instead of your usual stores. The purchase of even a single item from each parent conveys support and positive feelings regarding the fund raiser for your child and his/her school.

"Felix's Fund Raising Frenzy – Oops!"

"I can't believe how expensive this wrapping paper is! I can get it at Shopmart for a third the price!" Felix's mother complained when Felix brought home his first fund raising kit from school. He was so excited after attending the assembly that day when the project was introduced to the students. The school band played, the principal spoke and the PTA President challenged all classes to have 100% participation. Felix was excited about his name going in a raffle to win a daily prize for everyone who sold at least one item. Holiday season was approaching and Felix knew that his mother wrapped a lot of gifts each year and would need wrapping paper to do the job. But now his spirits were crushed – if his mother did not buy at least one roll of wrapping paper, would anyone buy from him? Felix remembered when his parents were still married and lived in a big house the next town over. It seemed every month a neighborhood student would come to the door selling candy bars, raffle tickets and even wrapping paper to support their school band and other clubs. Felix was fascinated and his dad always purchased something. Felix couldn't wait for his turn, and now that he was in second grade, he finally got a chance. But his chance was destroyed even before he began since his own mother wouldn't buy the wrapping paper. Felix decided to ask his dad when he came to pick him up tomorrow evening for their usual Wednesday evening visit, but when he did, his dad said that money was tight that month. He told Felix that he needed to understand that it was hard to keep up with all the bills and try to plan for a holiday vacation so not to bother with the fund raiser. Felix could not believe that his dad bought from every child in the neighborhood but would not buy from his own son! Didn't he understand that his class was trying to win the prize from the PTA? It was an ice cream party and everyone in his class had to sell at least one item. Felix had another idea – he could ask his grandmother. She loved him and would understand that this was important; after all, she used to be a teacher. But when Felix spoke to her, she said that people pay enough taxes to support schools and that the students did not need to raise money for schools. Lately, she was upset about a lot of things that happened at schools and Felix's dad explained that she was getting older and it was hard for her to accept how the world has changed. Maybe if he stayed absent from school next Friday when all the orders were due, his blank order form would not keep the class from earning the ice cream party, Felix thought.

"Frieda's Fund Raising Fun – WOW!"

Frieda had never won a prize in her life, but fifth grade was her lucky year! She really was not lucky that her parents got a divorce that year, but she felt lucky to have sold the highest number of candy bars in all the fifth grade classes for the entire school!! The girls' families of her Girl Scout troop all bought candy bars, her brother's basketball team and their families bought candy bars, the whole department at her mother's office and her father's auto dealership plus the customers bought candy bars, and Frieda even bought two for herself. In all, she sold 102 one dollar chocolate candy bars and managed to not lose a single dollar! Frieda used to lose her homework and other papers, but she managed to keep track of all the candy bar money this year. Her dad gave her a special tin box with a tiny lock and put the key on a purple ribbon, her favorite color. Together they decided to keep the box on her dresser at her dad's house and the key in the pencil cup on her desk. Every night after dinner, Frieda and her dad would count the money collected and list it on a special chart on the computer together. Frieda would type in the name of the person who bought the candy, how many each person bought, how much they paid her and she would add up the total amount collected each evening. Frieda's mom was away on a business trip for three weeks and Frieda was beginning to miss her more than ever. Each night, however, her mom would call at 8:30 in the evening and Frieda would tell her mom about her sales that day. Frieda's mom would tell Frieda about her day and that helped Frieda to not miss her mom so much. Her mom joked with her and said that it felt like she was one sales executive talking to another sales executive! This made Frieda beam with pride, because she knew her mother had a very important job at her business. She could not wait to go to her mom's office for "Take Your Daughter to Work Day" next month. Her parents decided that she would go with her mom this year since she went to her father's auto dealership last year. Frieda was glad she had two fantastic parents and thought maybe it was not so bad for them to be divorced after all. She knew they both loved her and were both so proud and excited for her to have won the first prize in her life for selling 102 chocolate candy bars for her school fund raiser.

---

*Important points to remember about your child's school fund raisers

Your child's school promotes the fund raising events, encouraging all students to participate in school wide activities. Support from both parents assists your child to feel connected to their school and feel that they are providing an important contribution. Several dollars towards an overpriced item is a small price to pay in order to promote your child's feelings of belonging. This is especially important for children whose parents are divorced, an experience that can challenge their sense of belonging.

Holiday Celebrations and Parties: Hazards or Happiness

*Why do schools have celebrations for holidays?

Class unity involves having fun together as well as learning together. Routines, rituals and celebrating holidays offer an opportunity for learning as well as fun. These classroom celebrations are anticipated excitedly and planned for by the entire class for several weeks ahead of time.

*Which parent should attend if parents are welcome?

Most classroom celebrations at the younger grade level are open to family members. If both parents are able to participate, your child will enjoy having both of you there.

*Should I bring my partner? Is it okay for my ex to bring his/her partner?

Generally classrooms are small and do not accommodate a large number of people. Seating is often crowded with adults sitting with their child in children's chairs. It might be more comfortable for your child to share this occasion with one or both parents; however, each celebration and family situation is different. Discuss this with your child's teacher if in doubt.

*How can we learn ahead of time when these celebrations will be scheduled?

An open house held at the beginning of the school year is the appropriate opportunity to ask about holiday celebrations planned for the school year by your child's teacher.

Chapter Fifteen: *Holiday Celebrations and Parties: Hazards or Happiness*

Is it important for our child to have us attend each celebration?

You know your child best. If a particular holiday celebration is very significant for him or her, it would be a good time for you to take off from work to attend. Discuss your work schedule with your child and child's teacher to determine which celebrations and school events would be most important for you to attend, if you are limited in time off from work.

What if I do not want to be in the same room as my ex or his/her partner?

Holiday celebrations in the classroom are about your child and unity with his/her class. Your child's feelings and sense of belonging are more important than your discomfort. In order to provide your child with the best opportunity to develop a positive self image, self confidence, and enjoyment of school, it is important for you to put your feelings as secondary to your child's needs for this as well as many school events. Suspend your discomfort for the short time, in order to benefit your child.

Which parent should pay for or send in requested contributions?

Children are often asked to contribute food, paper goods, or a gift for a gift exchange. Your child will be proud to contribute and may feel extremely embarrassed if not contributing. Either parent can provide this contribution; however, it is more convenient for the parent with whom the child stays with most of the time during the school week to take care of this. Most importantly, both parents should communicate to be sure this is not forgotten, as your child may feel very embarrassed if not contributing.

What is our child's responsibility regarding school holiday celebrations?

Your child is responsible to bring home any written flyers or invitations to his/her classroom holiday celebrations and discuss the arrangements with both joint custody parents. Your child is responsible to demonstrate appropriate behavior and polite manners at the celebration.

81

How can we make this a positive experience for our child?

Determine if this is an important event for your child and make arrangements for a family member to attend on your behalf if you are not able to go. Enjoy a relaxing time at your child's school, and take the opportunity to meet your child's classmates and their parents.

"Holly's Holiday Party Hazard – Oops!"

Holly's Kindergarten teacher had spent the entire month teaching the class about Christmas, Chanukah, Kwanza and several other cultural celebrations held in December. Holly was very excited to have learned the songs and make decorations for each holiday. She had a line to memorize for their classroom play being presented to the parents the last day of school before the winter break. Holly spent every day practicing her line and was proud to be chosen to speak. Several parents of the students were baking ethnic treats for their class celebration and the rest of the students were donating paper goods. Holly was to bring in paper cups for the drinks. She was confused about which nights she slept at her mom's and which nights she slept at her dad's house since their divorce last year. Every other week, she was at dad's Sunday through Wednesday, and then it reversed to her mom's house on those days, she thought. Holly couldn't figure out if the class celebration was on a day she was at her mom's or dad's house. She was not sure who to give the invitation to and who to ask to buy the cups. Every time she thought of it, Holly worried that her dad would be upset if she asked her mom or her mom would be upset if she asked her dad. Holly was not sure who to ask, but was very excited about the party. Holly's teacher reminded the class to bring their food and paper goods, as well as the classroom parent who was helping to coordinate the event. Holly was confused as to days of the week and didn't realize that Friday was here and it was the day of the class party. She burst out crying when she realized she did not have the paper cups. Even though the teacher tried to comfort her and assured her that there were paper cups in the teacher's lounge they could use, Holly felt so sad. When it was her turn to read her line, she was too upset and almost cried. She managed to recite the words: "happy and peaceful holiday to everyone", but had trouble

smiling while speaking. It was her first part in a class play and neither of her parents was there to see her. Holly's teacher smiled
proudly at her and told Holly how wonderful she was, but Holly
couldn't help but wish that both her parents had been there.

"Hubert's Holiday Party Happiness – WOW!"

Hubert's dad received a phone call from a woman who was the
classroom parent for Hubert's second grade class. She explained that
she was assisting the teacher to plan a Thanksgiving feast for the
students and their families. All family members were invited and
requested to bring a dish to share. Hubert's dad explained that
Hubert had two families including a mom, step dad, three step sisters, a dad, and his fiancée. He was relieved when the class parent
told him that they were all invited since the feast was to be held in
the cafeteria and there was enough room for everyone. He offered to
bring two desserts – one from him and one from Hubert's mother.
Hubert was accustomed to large Thanksgiving Day celebrations and
told everyone it was his favorite holiday. That is why Hubert's dad
knew that both he and his ex wife would make sure to be at this holiday party. He immediately phoned Hubert's mother to tell her about
the Thanksgiving Day celebration at school so she would have
enough time to arrange to take off from work. She was happy to
bring an apple pie, as Hubert's dad agreed to bring a pumpkin pie to
the party. Hubert was so excited that both families were attending,
but felt sorry for his best friend Steven, whose parents would not be
there. Steven once confided to Hubert that he was jealous of all the
fun times Hubert got to have with both of his families; it almost
didn't seem fair that Steven rarely got to spend time with his parents
who were not even divorced! Steven wished that he could sit at
Hubert's families' table for the Thanksgiving Day dinner instead of
the teacher's table with the other children whose parents could not
attend. Hubert had the same idea and decided to ask his parents, all
four of them. He smiled to himself because he knew what they
would say.

Important points to remember about your child's holiday parties

What might seem like a minor inconvenience to you could be a significant event for your child. School parties and celebrations are events which many children remember for years to come. Having you in their memory of the event can help promote a sense of security and normalcy, when having divorced parents can sometimes feel different and ungrounded. Help your child to develop special, happy memories, despite having to live with divorce.

Chapter Sixteen

Donations and Collections: Dungeons or Delight

*What is the purpose of collections and donations at school?

Collections of canned goods and other items are often conducted at schools to benefit low income families or families suffering from the after effects of a natural disaster such as a hurricane or flood. The purpose of this is to instill a sense of community service in students. Empathy for the feelings and needs of others less fortunate are promoted as part of the school's curriculum. Schools wish to contribute to the establishment of a greater sense of humanity in our country. Other collections might include classroom supplies such as boxes of tissues or items used in the classroom not supplied by the school district.

*Why do the schools have contests between classrooms for donations?

Classroom unity, feelings of belonging and community participation are the key elements addressed by contests for donations. Teachers may offer extra credit for participation in order to further promote community service and classroom pride.

*Where are these donations going?

Food, clothing, money and other donations are directed at organized charities which may be community based, or federally based. Careful research to determine the legitimacy of the selected charities is done by the teachers and school principal, and is generally monitored by the school district.

*How are the charities selected?

The selected charities are often based upon a local community need or an established not for profit organization which may be related to a cause being studied in your child's classroom or a well publicized need in our country. Victims of war and natural disaster are common needs that children can relate to.

Is it necessary for our child to participate in each collection or donation?

Collections and donations are generally voluntary; however it is in your child's best interests to participate. Your child may feel left out and uncomfortable if others are participating and classroom time is spent discussing the importance of the community need. Donations of a single canned food will cost less than one dollar, and is a valuable bargain in helping to contribute to your child's sense of community service.

Why does the teacher request donations of classroom supplies?

Some school districts do not provide enough funding for classroom supplies needed in the classroom. Boxes of tissues, art and craft supplies, and items needed for projects such as shoe boxes might be requested from families of students.

Which parent should pay for or send in the donations?

The cost of the donation is generally very small and either or both joint custody parent can supply this for your child's classroom.

What is our child's responsibilities regarding donations or collections?

Your child is responsible to bring home any written information regarding the donations being collected and discuss this with both joint custody parents. If no written information is supplied, your child is responsible for recording donation requests in his or her homework assignment book and making sure to give parents enough notice in order to avoid last minute crunches.

How can we help make this a positive learning experience for our child?

Classroom donations are a perfect opportunity for parents to promote a sense of empathy and community service in their children. Discussion involving those less fortunate and opportunities to help will flow naturally at home when classroom donations are requested. Parents are encouraged to be aware of various questions from curious young children regarding those less fortunate and older children regarding political issues in our country and our world which contribute to development of economic problems.

"Dwight's Donation Dungeon – Oops!"

Dwight's mom said: "I donate at the office" when he asked his mom for a can of food for the food drive at school. He knew that there were many cans of food in their pantry and just wanted to take one. There was a contest at his school and his fifth grade class was trying to get one hundred percent participation. But his mom told him to concentrate on his math homework since he was not doing very well in math. He wanted to explain about the food drive, but his mom was busy on the phone with his aunt. Since his parents got divorced six months ago, his mom was on the phone a lot with her friends and relatives. Sometimes he heard her talking about his dad and sometimes he saw her crying. Dwight knew that it was best to leave her alone and not bother her with anything at those times. Those times were happening a lot lately and Dwight missed seeing his mother happy. She was always very interested in Dwight's school projects and even was a classroom parent for several years. Since the divorce, Dwight's mother had to go back to work and was tired or sad most of the time. Maybe he would ask for the canned food tomorrow, but Thanksgiving was approaching soon and he needed to bring it to school by the end of the week. The food drive was for families who could not afford a Thanksgiving dinner. Maybe he should not ask his mom again at all, she might be sad to think of Thanksgiving without the whole family together with his dad. Dwight was sad about that but knew he had to pretend that he was fine so as not to worry his mother. Dwight decided to ask his father to help, but he was disappointed when his father did not pick him up for their usual Wednesday evening together. Dwight's father called him and said he had to work overtime that night. He explained to Dwight that he would have to work more overtime shifts after his parents got divorced in order to pay the bills. Dwight's dad lived in a small apartment and Dwight didn't understand why there were so many bills to pay, but he did hear his parents arguing about money and wondered if it was his fault when he overheard his mom say how expensive it was to raise a child. Dwight didn't tell his teacher why he didn't have a can of food for the food drive and he didn't tell her how he worried about his mom and was sad about not seeing his dad. His teacher said he was day-dreaming a lot lately and that was why he was doing poorly in math. When the winner of the classroom contest was announced, Dwight tried to pretend that he was not listening, but he knew that it was his fault that his class did not win.

"Diana's Donation Delight – WOW!"

"Did you know that there are children who do not have toys to play with?" asked Diana when she arrived home from Kindergarten one day. Her mom explained that not all families can afford to buy children toys like she has, but when Diana's teacher discussed it in class, Diana gave it more thought. She wanted to help these children and was so glad that her teacher told her how she can do it. Diana asked her mom if they could go to the discount store in town and purchase a toy for a young girl or boy for Diana to take to school for the donation being collected in her classroom. Her mom explained that the trip to the toy store would not be for her and that Diana was not to ask for a toy for herself during their shopping. Even though Diana said she understood, it was hard for her to not ask her mother to buy her the newest collecting cards at the counter that she wanted so much. But, Diana kept her promise and it was worth it when her mom told her how proud she was. After all, it was not fair for her to get something new when other children did not have any new toys. The next day at school, Diana was excited to bring the new doll she selected to her teacher and help wrap it for a holiday gift for a girl who didn't have any dolls. Diana wished she could be friends with this girl and play with her sometime with her new doll. But her teacher explained that donations are anonymous. When Diana asked her mother more questions about how it could be that some children did not have toys or even enough food to eat, Diana's mother brought her to their church to show her other ways they could make a difference in the lives of others less fortunate. Even though Diana's mother and father were divorced, Diana's mother told her dad about Diana's good deed. The next time Diana went to her dad's house, he showed her pictures of a local community that was devastated by floods with many families losing their homes. Diana had an idea. Maybe her father would take her to the toy store so she could buy a doll for a girl who lost hers in the flood. She promised her dad that she would not ask for a toy for herself, even though she knew how hard it would be to keep her promise. Diana was surprised at how good it felt to help someone that she did even know and knew how proud both of her parents were of her. Most of all, she felt good about herself.

---

*Important points to remember about your child's donations

Both parents can take the opportunity to instill a sense of community service and empathy for others when your child's school is having a collection for a charity. Both parents can also take the time to have discussions with older children about political awareness in the world and locally in order to communicate values and encourage an interest in local and world affairs. This will enhance your child's self esteem as well as promote a healthy intervention to respond to depression. Helping others has been reported by many to improve a sense of well being by focusing on the needs of others when one is feeling sad, lonely and unable to change their situation. Clues to developing a healthy sense of self and intervention to respond to depression are indeed hidden in a school charity drive. Don't miss this important opportunity for your child!

Chapter Seventeen

Contests: Caverns or Celebrations

Why does the school have contests for children?
Competition can inspire and motivate children towards participating in an assignment or event. Children who do not excel in academic grades have an opportunity to be recognized for other talents such as writing skills, music, art, athletics or citizenship. Class unity, team spirit and the responsibility in working with others is an important experience for learning to maintain a job as an adult.

What type of contests are held yearly at schools?
Which organizations sponsor removed space contests at schools?
Many opportunities to enter contests are available on a school wide basis, including community, local, statewide and the national level. Poster and writing contests regarding specific topics are popular, as well as academic and citizenship contests. Your child's teacher may nominate your child if they demonstrate a particular strength.

How can we learn ahead of time which contests will be held each school year?
The school newsletter or website announces contests, as well as notices sent home with your child. You may see posters at your child's school announcing such contests or communicate with your child's teacher to learn of these opportunities.

Is it necessary for our child to participate in every contest?
It would be impractical for your child to participate in every contest available; however, you may wish to encourage your child to partici-

pate in contests which address their special talents. It is also important to your child to participate in contests which are class wide in order to experience the feeling of class unity and not feel left out.

Which parent should assist our child in participation?

Both joint custody parents can encourage and assist your child in contest participation.

What is our child's responsibility in participating in school contests?

Your child is responsible to bring home notices and inform both joint custody parents of contests being offered at school. Your child is responsible to participate in class wide contests and be a responsible team player when with a group.

How can we help make this a positive experience for our child?

In addition to encouraging your child to participate in contests which address a special talent or skill your child possesses, both parents can take the opportunity to teach your child to be a good sport and not a sore loser. Accepting compliments and learning to accept not winning while being inspired to try again is just as important as congratulating their classmates who win.

"Carol's Contest Caverns – Oops!"

Carol was interested in applying for an essay contest that her eighth grade Language Arts teacher told the class about. She had received several A's on her written essays that semester and was thinking of applying to a high school in her community that offered a special program in journalism. Carol was not that interested in school this year since her parents got divorced. She was not that interested in much of anything, but found solace in pouring her feelings into her written journal. Carol had no idea that she would be able to explain the many upsetting and confusing feelings she was having that year. It was hard to talk about, but the written words flowed naturally for her. Carol showed her work to her teacher and was relieved to hear that it was indeed well written. The topic of the essay for the contest was about overcoming a challenge. Could Carol write about her cross country move three years ago, the grief over the death of her brother, or about the feelings of confusion and loneliness when her parents divorced? Any of those topics would be acceptable, her Language Arts teacher told her, but she did need permission from her parents to enter the contest. Carol had not told either of her parents about her feelings; she only had written them in her journal. Although it was never expressed directly to Carol by either of her parents, it was clear that she was not supposed to talk about her feelings. "Just move on", was the motto Carol was taught. But how can she move on when the court proceedings were still happening. Carol overheard her parents arguing and once even saw a legal document about how her parents were supposed to handle money matters. Why did it take more than a year to resolve this? Carol could not ask anyone, but she could write in her journal. When her essay was complete, Carol typed it on the word processor on the computer, the night before it was due. She hadn't meant to wait until the last minute, but was wary about asking her mom or dad to sign for permission; they both seemed so preoccupied in their work, part of that "moving on" philosophy, Carol thought. The printer broke down just as Carol was about to print her essay. She called her father and asked if she could come over his house and print it that night, but he was too busy to pick her up. Her mom already said no to taking her to the local office supply store to get a disk to save it to so she could print it at school. Would her mom really understand how important this was to Carol, even if she could explain it to her? Besides, Carol's mother was waiting for Carol to finish using the computer so she could get on it for her job. Carol really wanted to tell her mom about how important this was to her, but she didn't even know how to begin. Wasn't a mother just supposed to know how her daughter feels? Didn't Carol's mother even read Carol's journal that she left out on her desk secretly hoping her mother would take a peek? Maybe it was not such a good idea to enter a writing contest after all, Carol thought. She didn't need to study journalism in high school, anyway. Carol didn't really care about the essay contest anymore, or much of anything else for that matter.

"Charles Contest Celebrations – WOW!"

Charles teacher called him up to her desk and told him about a poster contest being sponsored by the school cafeteria on good nutrition. Mrs. Culbert, Charles' fourth grade teacher noticed that he always brought a nutritious lunch packed from home and when she commented to him about it once, Charles told her that he made his own lunches for school every evening! Since his parents got divorced last year, his mom had to work longer hours and asked him to help out at home. She taught him to pack his lunch and Charles was surprised that other children did not pack their own lunch. Although Charles struggled to achieve C's in writing and math, he always got A's in art class and his art teacher told him he had a special talent. Still, Charles never entered a contest before and was apprehensive about participating. His best friend, Sam, who always got all A's, told him to go for it, so he asked his mom. She liked the idea so he also asked his dad. Charles' dad offered to take him to an art supply store for the poster board and new markers for his project and allowed him to keep it set up on the kitchen table for the entire weekend visit. It was kind of fun eating on snack tables with his dad anyway and he loved working on his poster. His dad insisted on taking a picture of Charles' poster and Charles wondered if Sam's parents ever took a picture of his all A's report card. Probably not, he decided. When it was complete, he brought it home to his mom's house on Sunday evening and she wrapped it clear plastic wrap in case it rained on the way to school. Even though Charles had been taking the bus to school each day, his mom arranged to get to work late so she could drive him in with his poster for the contest. Charles was the only student in his class to enter and the teacher as well as the students oohed and aahed when they saw his poster. Maybe he was great at something after all, even if it was not writing or math. Charles won second place in the poster contest at his school and he was excited to receive a red ribbon with gold lettering. His entire class applauded and cheered for him when the winners were announced on the loudspeaker one morning. His poster as well as the first place winner's was sent to the district office to be displayed and participate in a district wide contest. Charles didn't mind if he won the district contest or not, he already felt like a winner.

*Important points to remember about your child's school contests

Your child develops self esteem by determining what they excel in. Trying out different activities helps them identify their strengths. Contests are an important opportunity to identify and recognize special talents which are not as obvious as academic grades. For example, participating in an art or writing contest will enhance your child's self esteem, whether or not they do win. Parents can take the opportunity to teach positive social skills for winners and losers and encourage your child to try again despite not winning.

Chapter Eighteen

Discipline / Referrals / Detentions / Suspensions: Ditches or Dazzle

How can we learn about our child's school discipline policy?
The school's discipline policy is explained in detail in The Student Code of Conduct Handbook provided to students at most schools. Generally, both the parents and the student are required to sign having received a copy of this policy and agreement to comply with all school rules.

What is a referral?
After a verbal warning to students who do not follow the school or classroom rules, the teacher will complete a written document detailing the problem and forward it to the school administrator responsible for discipline. This document is known as a "referral".

What is detention?
A common consequence given to students who violate school rules is having the student arrive to school early, stay after school or attend on a Saturday to serve what is known as "detention".

What is an in school suspension?
One level of consequence in many schools is to have the child serve a detention during the school day, in a room where they must do their assigned work and remain quiet, away from the rest of their class.

What is suspension?
Suspension is when a student is required to remain home from school for the consequence of not following the school rules.

What is an alternative to suspension program?

Some school districts offer an alternative location away from the school for suspended students to attend during their suspension from school for violation of school rules.

What is mediation?

Many schools have found that by mediating interpersonal conflicts which occur between students, they can avoid referrals and suspensions. Typical student problems which are handled in mediation are name calling, gossip, rumor passing and fights. Students involved agree to be respectful to each other and discontinue all inappropriate behaviors addressed. Students are often trained to be peer mediators, a formalized program which has had a high success rate.

Which parent will the school contact if our child has had disciplinary action?

The administrator handling a discipline referral will generally contact the first name on the list of guardians and continue to attempt to reach a parent on the list using all phone numbers provided.

Which parent should attend a discipline meeting at school?

It sends a powerful message of your unified expectations that your child follow all school rules if both joint custody parents attend a discipline meeting at your child's school.

Do parents have further recourse if we believe the disciplinary action is unfair?

The first actions for a parent to take if it is felt that your child is being treated unfairly is to calmly and politely state your concern to the administrator, focusing on the facts. Very often, an administrator is willing to see the situation in a different light and reconsider a consequence if it is felt that the parent is supporting the school rules. If you are not satisfied with the response, the school principal is the next step, then the district office. Keep documentation of meetings with the school for your records.

What if parents disagree with each other on how to manage the disciplinary action?

It is common for married parents as well as joint custody divorced parents to have a different philosophy on discipline at home as well as at school. It is also normal for children to attempt to follow their own rules and avoid consequences for doing so. Children with joint custody divorced parents have a greater opportunity to manipulate the disagreeing parents to avoid focusing on the fact that they broke a school rule and were caught. In order to develop a sense of responsibility in your child, it is imperative that parents discuss, compromise and present a united front to your child regarding your expectation of complying with all school rules.

Should parents add an additional consequence at home for our child?

The decision regarding whether an additional home consequence is added, as well as what the consequence will be should be discussed and agreed upon by both joint custody parents. Every situation and every child is different and there is no one advisable policy to follow. Consider together if the school consequence is enough to impart an important learning experience for your child. For further guidelines as to how to respond to school discipline, consult your child's school Guidance Counselor for a professional opinion, however, do not lose sight of the fact that parents know their child best.

Should a parent take off form work to supervise an at home suspension?
Which parent should be responsible to supervise an at home suspension?

Most parents would rather take off from work to attend a positive school function to support their children rather than supervising an at home suspension. Depending upon the child, supervision might be necessary in order to provide a safe environment which will deter further breaking of rules by your child. Joint custody parents might try to share this responsibility, as well as relying on relatives for assistance.

What is our child's responsibility regarding school discipline?

Your child is responsible to know the school rules and abide by them at all times. If a rule is broken, your child is responsible to tell the truth about it, be respectful to the administrator in charge of discipline and serve the consequence.

How can we help our child learn to be responsible regarding the school rules?

Joint custody divorced parents can make a concerted effort to convey to their children the expectation that all school rules be followed at all times, by presenting this expectation as a united front. Discussions regarding the importance of these rules can be conducted at your child's level, depending upon the age and level of maturity.

"David's Discipline Ditches – Oops!"

David's best friend Stephanie didn't mean to let other students in the high school lunchroom see what she found in David's backpack – a bottle of beer he took from his father's house, but it somehow got passed around the lunch table when she was going through his backpack as a joke that Friday afternoon. The Assistant Principal was standing right there and David was busted!! David knew that he was not supposed to bring any alcohol to school, but it was just a high school prank, he never intended to drink it at lunch in school. Mr. Weiss could not take a joke – something about a zero tolerance policy, and David was getting worried that he was really in trouble. David knew his dad would understand since he was a prankster himself. Certainly David's mom would be angry, she was always angry at his dad's pranks which is why they finally divorced. David explained to Mr. Weiss that his parents were divorced and had joint custody so it would be best to call his dad when he learned that a parent had to be notified. David could hear his dad laughing on the other end of the telephone as Mr. Weiss was explaining the situation. Whew! David was right; his dad did think it was funny. He could also overhear his dad suggesting to Mr. Weiss that David just be given a warning since he was a good student and no one actually drank any alcohol. But Mr. Weiss gave David a five day suspension and told him that he was lucky to not be expelled from school for the rest of the school year! David was with his mother most school nights but managed to keep the suspension scheduled for next week a secret from her. All weekend long, David spoke with his dad who promised to "turn things around" by speaking to the school principal. David's dad was not able to go to the school Monday morning since he had an important meeting at work. David's mother drove him to school as she had done every morning and David decided to just attend class as if nothing happened and assumed his father would speak to the principal that day and clear up this "misunderstanding." That turned out to not be a good plan, as David's first hour teacher sent David directly to Mr. Weiss' office. Mr. Weiss phoned David's mother this time and explained that it was required for a parent to come to school to pick David up personally. When David's mother arrived, David just wanted to leave quickly, but his mother had a long talk with the principal in which she explained that David's father was irresponsible and possibly an alcoholic! This embarrassed David so much that he could not look directly at Mr. Weiss. His mother assured the Assistant Principal that she would handle this at home and understood the suspension policy very clearly. She even thanked him!! David knew that he and his father would have a good laugh about how ridiculous this whole thing was. Maybe tomorrow, his dad would be able to straighten this out with the principal, David thought.

"Dina's Discipline Dazzle – WOW!"

Dina's arm hurt where Rita, the classroom bully had punched her, after Dina had slapped Rita for calling her names. She just could not take being called fat and stupid one more time, so she slapped Rita across the face on the school playground. Next thing she knew, Rita punched her in the arm and their fourth grade teacher, Mrs. Nelson, was there in a split second to break it up. Both girls were now in the principal's office and parents were immediately phoned. Dina had not told her parents that she was being called names at school. Dina's parents had just divorced and she didn't think they would listen anyway. Both of her parents always told her to ignore rude classmates, which is exactly what Dina was trying to do, but it just finally got to her and she couldn't contain herself. Dina had never hit anyone before and Mrs. Nelson was surprised. Dina was even more surprised at herself for doing so. Within the hour, both Dina's parents arrived at school and Dina explained the name calling and the hitting. Mrs. Nelson called in the school Guidance Counselor to help resolve the problem between Dina and Rita. Both girls apologized and both were given after school detention for two days. Dina's mother and father said they wanted to have a talk with her when they were finished meeting with the principal. They all went back to Dina's mother's house for the talk. Dina knew she was really in trouble since her dad had always picked her up at the door when he came for their visitation, never coming in the house since the divorce. But, Dina was wrong. She was not in further trouble at all. Both her parents told her how much they loved her and how she should never keep a problem from them again, no matter how small it seemed. Just because they were divorced, she should still know that she was very important to both of them and she should never forget that. Dina knew she should not have slapped Rita, and was relieved that she was not in further trouble at home.

Important points to remember about your child's school discipline

Adult rules such as workplace, paying bills and obeying traffic laws are accompanied with consequences for not complying with them. Learning to obey school rules and serve consequences for not doing so prepares your child for their future life in the adult world. Do not prevent your child from learning responsibility through experiencing consequences at school for disobeying a school rule. Divorced, joint custody parents should present a united front to their children regarding their expectations that all school rules be followed.

Chapter Nineteen

Course Selections: Snowstorms or Sundaes

At which grade does our child get to select his/her courses?

While course selection varies between school districts, the first opportunity to make a choice for an elective course generally is at the Middle School level or sixth grade.

What are the differences between the academic levels?

Courses are taught at different paces, with different levels of difficulty and in depth exploration, depending upon the academic ability and achievement of the students. Remedial classes are for students who have difficulty grasping the concepts or are behind grade level. Advanced, gifted and honors level classes proceed at a greater speed, go more in depth into the topic being covered and require higher level assignments.

How will the school determine which level is appropriate for our child?

Standardized test scores as well as past achievement will be used to determine the level of coursework which is most appropriate for your child.

What if parents disagree with the school's assessment of our child's ability?

Parents can request a meeting with your child's teacher and Guidance Counselor to review your child's ability, performance and best current level of coursework. Being open minded in listening to the schools' rationale for the appropriate selection will promote the school personnel to be open minded in listening to the parents.

What if parents disagree with each other?

Your child may feel confused and unsure of him/herself if joint custody parents disagree openly about his/her abilities and proper school placement. Parents should discuss their concerns with each other, examine the facts, consult with your child's teacher and or Guidance Counselor and come to a compromise. Your child will feel more secure with a united front from his or her parents.

How can we learn what the required courses are for graduation?

Graduation requirements are established by each state and interpreted by each school district. Your child's Guidance Counselor will monitor your child's schedule to be sure that required courses are taken throughout their high school career. See the Guidance Counselor for a list of requirements for graduation.

What are electives?

Electives are courses that your child has a selection of based upon their special interests and the availability at your child's school. These are in addition to traditional reading, math, language arts, social studies and science. A specific number of electives are required for graduation and your child has a selection of special interests in the arts, music, journalism and many vocational interests.

How much responsibility should our child have in selecting his/her schedule?

Most schools require the parent to sign their child's course selection which demonstrates an expectation that parents be included in the selection process.

What are the alternatives if our child fails a grade or a course?

Some school districts offer summer school, evening school and online courses. Check with your child's school Guidance Counselor for the available options in your district.

Do parents get to decide if their child should repeat a grade?
What if both parents disagree on whether our child should repeat the grade?

Decisions regarding retention are carefully made using a specific criteria developed by your child's school district. Parents are generally notified early on and given opportunities for remediation if their child is in danger of repeating a grade. Input from parents is encouraged but parents are generally not in a position to reverse a school's decision regarding retention.

Which parent should decide how to manage making up a failed course?

Options regarding repeating failed courses should be discussed by both joint custody parents along with your child and your child's Guidance Counselor. Pros and cons of each option should be reviewed and a decision made together based upon your child's abilities and your family's specific situation.

What is our child's responsibility in selecting courses or repeating a grade?

Your child is responsible to learn the course requirements for their grade and for graduation, discuss options with their school Guidance Counselor and with both joint custody parents.

How can we help our child learn to be responsible for passing the grade/course?

Monitoring organizations skills, study skills and motivation, along with healthy eating and sleeping habits will provide the best possible opportunity for your child to be responsible and develop maturity regarding school. Both joint custody parents will have the highest success in teaching responsibility to their child if they keep in contact with each other to discuss concerns and changes in their child's daily habits and school progress.

"Sybil's Course Selection Snowstorm – Oops!"

Sybil was very excited to attend the eighth grade assembly at her middle school one morning when she learned that the high school she would be going to next year was there to present information about their school.

Sybil wanted to study journalism and her high school offered elective courses with a state of the arts studio to broadcast their morning announcements. Sybil knew that her mother wanted her to take business courses so she could be assured of a marketable skill and a good job after graduation even though Sybil was not interested in business. Why couldn't she just study what she wanted! Sybil's dad was insisting that she take additional math and science classes to help her get into a great college and her mom and dad openly disagreed about their plans for Sybil. This was no surprise since they disagreed about everything which was probably why they got divorced when Sybil was very young. They had joint custody and Sybil had a close relationship with both of them, but she was beginning to feel like they were both pulling her in two different directions when they talked about her future. Sybil respected both of her parents' opinions and was not really sure who was right, but she did know that she wanted the opportunity to decide about her own future. When the course selection cards came out, there was a place for a parent signature and all the students were encouraged to discuss their choices with their parents. No one knew how difficult of a task this was for Sybil. There was only room for one elective in ninth grade and Sybil wanted to take beginning Journalism. Her mom wanted her to take Business and her dad insisted on an additional math class. Sybil's Guidance Counselor explained that the course selection cards were due in one week. Sybil didn't really want to explain to the Guidance Counselor that her parents disagreed; she hated even thinking about it. Maybe she should just take the course her parents wanted her to and wait until she was an adult to do what she wanted. But which parent should she listen to? If she took mom's advice, Dad would be angry and if she took dad's advice, mom would be hurt. Maybe she could just leave it blank and take what the computer selects, which is what the Guidance Counselor explained would happen. Or maybe Sybil could just hand in the card with her Journalism choice and no parent signature and hope it is not missed. That wouldn't really be lying, would it? Sybil wondered.

"Steven's Course Selection Sundae – WOW!"

Steven was not sure whether to take advanced classes or regular classes for his ninth grade schedule. Colleges look at the difficulty level of coursework when deciding who to admit he was told. But Steven also knew he might have trouble keeping up his grades in advanced classes and colleges most certainly considered grades. His mother thought about it and came up with a good plan. She was always a good planner, considering all the possibilities, except for when she and Steven's dad divorced. His mother had not planned for that, Steven was sure of since he overheard her telephone conversations and his parent's fights last year. But, as promised, Steven got to spend time with both parents and they explained to him that joint custody meant both parents participated in decision making about important events in his life. His high school course selection was one of these important events. Steven's mother scheduled an appointment for Steven, his mom and his dad to meet with the high school Guidance Counselor to learn of the pros and cons of the different course selections. All three of them listened carefully as the available options were listed. Both his parents then turned to Steven and asked him what he thought and what he wanted to do. Steven really wanted his parents to make the decision for him so he would not be responsible if it was the wrong decision, but he knew that they would both insist that it was his decision. The option of taking advanced classes in his strongest subjects, language arts and science was the final choice Steven made, with the possibility of transferring to advanced classes in his other subjects after he settled into his first year of high school. Steven was glad they met with the Guidance Counselor. He did not know that he had all these options. He wondered why his parents divorced, but was more preoccupied with looking forward to going to high school next year.

> **Important points to remember about your child's course selections*
>
> As with any decisions, the best process to follow is to get all the information, discuss the various options along with pros and cons and make a decision as a team regarding the most positive opportunity for your child.

Chapter Twenty

Career Day: Crashes or Champs

*What is Career Day?

Some schools set aside a day each year to introduce their students to various career choices by meeting parents and individuals in the community from different careers.

*How can I learn when Career Day is scheduled at our child's school?

Inquire with the Guidance Department or your child's teacher at the beginning of the school year. You may also check the school calendar which some schools now have posted online.

*Should I participate in Career Day?

If you have a career that you really enjoy and are proud of, it would be a great benefit to the students at your child's school to hear about your experience.

*What if my ex is also participating?

Your participation should be based upon whether you have something to offer young people by informing them about your career experience. Speakers are generally placed in different rooms throughout the day, or classes revolve throughout the room you present in. If a complimentary lunch is offered, you can sit with one of the other participants.

*Is it okay for my partner to participate in Career Day?

If your child is comfortable with your partner participating, and your partner has an interesting career that (s)he is proud of and enjoys, then participation is a great idea.

Would our child want me to participate in Career Day?

Ask your child about their feelings about your participation. If you enjoy your career and are proud of it, chances are that your child will be pleased to have you share your experience with others at their school.

Why are the benefits to me and our child of my participation in Career Day?

Students often comment to the child of the presenter about how cool it might be to have a parent with your career. Your child has an opportunity to make more friends by having another topic of conversation to discuss with their peers. As a Career Day speaker, your contribution will be appreciated by the school staff and you will have an opportunity to get to know administration, teachers and students at your child's school.

What are the benefits to our child's school of my participation?

Students at your child's school will have a first hand opportunity to hear about the various job opportunities in your chosen career and hear of your personal experience in this career as well as how to prepare for this career. As a role model, you will be influencing many young people as well as recruiting interest in your chosen profession.

What is our child's responsibility regarding Career Day?

Your child is responsible to bring home any notices about Career Day and show it to both joint custody parents. Your child is responsible to treat you and the other speakers with respect and courtesy when attending the Career Day presentations.

"Cedric's Career Day Crash – Oops!"

Cedric wanted his dad to participate in his school's Career Day but wasn't sure if it was such a good idea. His parents had recently gotten divorced and Cedric's dad always seemed angry at Cedric's mom. Cedric's mom didn't seem to like it when Cedric had a fun time with his dad or if his dad bought him something. Cedric was almost eleven years old and was beginning to feel old enough to be pals with his dad. Just because his mom and dad didn't get along well, why couldn't he enjoy his dad? Once he overheard his mom telling a friend that Cedric's dad did not deserve his son's love and attention. So Cedric knew that if he asked his dad to talk about being a policeman to Cedric's fifth grade, his mom would be angry again. When Cedric's teacher specifically asked Cedric to check with his dad, Cedric thought that he found a way out of upsetting his mom. He couldn't have been more wrong, however, when his mom clearly showed her anger at the idea that his teacher would want Cedric's dad to help. Of course, Cedric's dad agreed to participate and seemed excited about it. When Career Day finally arrived, Cedric's mother was quiet and but kept sighing, rolling her eyes and shaking her head back and forth. Cedric wondered why she hated him so much, but when he once asked her, his mom told him that he would find out when he got older. Cedric wondered if his dad had other girlfriends while he was married to his mom. His dad was so handsome and girls always were talking to him and laughing with him. His mother didn't laugh much. Cedric was so proud to hear his father tell his class about being a policeman, but couldn't allow himself to be happy because he felt that he was being disloyal to his mother. He thought he saw his father flirting with his friend Billy's mother who was recently divorced as well. Maybe his mother was right – maybe his father did do something so terrible that he wasn't allowed to know about until he got older – but why was it a secret?

Billy was trying to enjoy the presenters at Career Day but was too worried about his parents to pay attention.

"Caryn's Career Day Champ - WOW!"

Caryn's mother was so proud that her thirteen year old daughter thought she was cool enough to ask her to participate in her school's Career Day. She always felt guilty working long hours getting her children's clothing store off the ground and having to take Caryn to work with her on weekends while she was growing up. Caryn told her mother that the teacher requested all types of professions to be represented and Caryn immediately raised her hand when the teacher specified business owner. Well, she was the owner of the business and she did build it from the ground up and was very proud of it. Caryn was truly proud of her mother and knew first hand about all the work that went into opening and running a business. At times, Caryn did resent it, but lately really seemed to appreciate the store and often came up with great marketing ideas. Caryn was looking forward to working in the store setting up displays and helping customers next summer. At least for half the summer; Caryn would be staying with her father for one month this summer as she had been doing for the past five summers since her parents divorced. She missed her mom during that month but had fun with her dad and enjoyed traveling with him on vacation. Although her parents had joint custody, Caryn's visitation with her dad was not on a regular schedule. He was a pilot and had irregular work hours. Caryn was planning on asking him to participate at Career Day but she knew that he did not know his schedule that far in advance. Caryn's mom came up with the idea of asking the school if her father could speak at Career Day only if he could schedule it at the last minute. The school was happy to accommodate him and her dad was willing to participate which meant that Caryn might actually have two parents helping out – Wow! Even though her parents were divorced, Caryn felt very lucky to have two parents who loved her and cared about her. And even though she was thirteen, Caryn felt that her parents were both cool and was happy.

*****Important points to remember about your child's school's Career Day**

Career Day is a rare opportunity for you to touch the lives of other children if you feel proud of yourself and your professional accomplishments. These positive feelings are extended to your child. Do not prevent your child from feeling proud of your ex, even if you are not.

Chapter Twenty-One

Post High School Planning: Puzzles or Payments

When does our child's school begin to address post graduation planning?

High Schools consider a student's plan for after high school when advising which high school courses to enroll in throughout their high school career. Certain courses are geared toward students planning on enrolling in college, while other courses are geared toward students planning on vocational training. Many high schools today offer extensive vocational training which lead to a certification in their chosen field.

Which school professionals are involved in planning for post graduation?

Your child's school Guidance Counselor will advise your child of opportunities and options available as well as helping to evaluate your child's abilities for success.

What opportunities are available for our child besides college?

Many more career opportunities are available today as our society has experienced advances in technology, medicine, agriculture, entertainment as well as other industries. Your child's school Guidance Department can direct you and your child to resources which describe these opportunities.

How can we learn of the available opportunities for our child?

Your child's school Guidance Counselor is only one contact to learn of opportunities. Be creative and arrange for your child to speak with friends, family members, neighbors and members of the community to learn of various career opportunities. Personnel departments in major companies in your community will be happy to talk with your child about available opportunities. Medical personnel in your child's physician's office and specialist's office are also good resources. Be aware of Career Fairs offered in your community.

How can we learn about college scholarships?

Some high schools have an advisor specifically designated to inform students and their families about college opportunities and scholarships. Many major organizations and companies offer scholarships for college as well. Be wary of solicitations from unscrupulous agencies offering college scholarships.

Which parent should assist in planning for after graduation?
Which parent should help select colleges our child will apply for?

Both joint custody divorced parents should assist their child in planning for after high school graduation. This is an example of the spirit of the joint custody agreement.

What if parents disagree with each other on college selections?

Joint custody parents can assist their child in determining the qualities, location, size and price range best suited for college choices. Your child's best interest and personal preference should guide your opinion. Be careful to not allow your feelings about your ex spouse to distort your assessment on what is best for your child.

Which parent will pay for our child's college?

College expenses are often specifically addressed in a divorce decree. If not agreed upon at the time of divorce, each parent must evaluate their values and available income they are willing to commit to college for their child. A combination of contributions from both parents and their child may be the best option.

What is our child's responsibility in planning for his/her future?

Your child is responsible to consider and discuss all options with an open mind. Your child is responsible to bring home and share with both joint custody parents any information provided by the school or mailed to them directly. Your child is responsible to be aware of timelines and deadlines in applying to colleges and vocational schools.

What can we do to help our child to be responsible to plan for after graduation?

Both joint custody parents can find opportunities to discuss plans for after high school with their child throughout the normal day to day conversations. A single conversation in their senior year will not be sufficient to help motivate most children to consider their future.

"Patty's Post High School Planning Puzzle – Oops!"

Patty had studied hard her entire school career and earned high grades as a result. She also participated in community volunteer projects with her church and school clubs, not because she knew it would be good for her college applications, but because she enjoyed doing so. Now that it was time to apply for colleges, Patty was unsure of how much her college education would cost. Her friends discouraged her from applying for loans and scholarships, telling her that her parents made too much money so she would not qualify. Her parents were divorced and she was unsure if both of their incomes would be included in determining eligibility. Money was a touchy subject for Patty and her family. Her dad had recently lost his business and her mom worked extra overtime hours to cover bills. No one ever talked to Patty about money; it was as if it was a forbidden topic. But Patty knew she had to approach the subject of college expenses with her parents so she finally had a talk with her mother. Patty was relieved when her mother informed her that it was always the plan for her dad to pay for her college expenses. Patty wondered if it was okay to discuss this with him directly and her mom encouraged her to. Patty was still visiting with her dad every other weekend and Wednesday evenings since her parents divorced ten years ago. One Wednesday evening at dinner Patty finally got up the courage to ask her father about college expenses. She could tell he was embarrassed and gave a vague answer about everything working out. But Patty needed to know whether she could apply for private colleges or only the state schools. Even the applications were expensive. Each school had their own financial aid application and there was a generic government application to complete as well for aid.

Patty's parents never discussed finances with her and she was afraid to ask them about their income and tax return. Patty showed the application to her mother since that was her primary residential home, even though her parents shared joint custody. Her mother told her to have her father complete the form since he was going to take care of college expenses. Patty's heart sank when she overheard her father on a telephone conversation to his brother saying he had to declare bankruptcy and didn't know how to explain to his daughter that he had no money for her college expenses. Patty knew she couldn't ask her mother since her mother didn't appear to have enough money each month to pay the bills. Finally, in desperation, Patty went to see her Guidance Counselor at school. Her Guidance Counselor had good and bad news: there were many college scholarships and loans available to Patty but the deadline for applying for many of them had already passed. Patty wondered why she ever listened to her friends and wondered if she would ever get to go to college.

"Perry's Post High School Planning Payment – WOW!"

Perry's dad was an auto mechanic and made a good income working for a car dealership. Perry always liked to visit his dad at the shop, and did so every weekend even after his parents divorced when he was eleven. His mom noticed that Perry not only enjoyed spending time with his dad, but enjoyed repairing everything around the house. Fortunately, he was also skilled at repairs. His relatives and neighbors would bring over small appliances for Perry to fix or just tinker with, and Perry spent most of his spare time in his own makeshift workshop in the garage. High school was difficult for Perry, but he did receive an A in a computer repair course he took during his senior year. Perry's mother said he had magic hands and could repair anything! Once, his best friend Brian wondered out loud if Perry could repair an airplane. That thought remained in Perry's mind when he was considering what trade school to go to after high school. His mother was thinking the same thing and had sent away to a program for information about their airplane repair training program. Even though Perry's parents were divorced, they mostly agreed about Perry, so it was no surprise that his dad had also sent away for information about a training program for computer repairs. Perry wondered what else he could repair and his neighbor talked to him about his job of repairing air conditioners. Perry's mom started a file on all training programs that offered a certificate in repairs, although she did not understand much about the field. That's where his dad could help. Perry and his dad reviewed all the programs that his mom had received information about. Each week, various brochures would arrive in the mail, and every weekend after Perry visited his dad at his job, he and his dad reviewed the programs and discussed if Perry might like it and how they compared to what he already knew. Perry's mom, the organized one of his parents, phoned the programs and arranged tours for six different programs in the community. Most of the time, both Perry's parents attended with him. Perry knew that they alternated taking time off from work so they both could be there for him and it made him feel very good to know how important he was to both of them. His friend Brian was already accepted at several top colleges in the state, but was not sure what he wanted to study. Perry felt lucky to have a skill that he could turn into a job, even though it felt like a hobby! Perry also felt very lucky to have two parents who loved him very much.

Important points to remember about your child's after high school planning

Parents can encourage their children to explore their interests, talents and skills throughout their entire educational career. The focus on exploration, without having to immediately choose a career makes the information more interesting and less overwhelming. Conversations about various careers and jobs can be approached on a natural day to day basis as your child comes in contact with various people throughout their day.

Chapter Twenty-Two

After School Sponsored Extra Curricular Activities, Clubs and Sports: Aftershocks or Aces

How can we learn which clubs are offered after school?

The student handbook provided at the beginning of the school year will list after school clubs and programs being offered at school. As additional ones are added, they are often advertised in the school newsletter, website and with posters displayed around campus.

Are all clubs that meet at the school sponsored by the school?

Sometimes the school allows community organizations, such as Girl Scouts, to use the school facility for club meetings. Most clubs, however, are sponsored by the school.

How can we decide which clubs our child should participate in?

Joining after school clubs gives your child an opportunity to explore various interests, enhance their strengths and make friends. Select a club which will encourage exploration of your child's interests and/or strengths.

Which parent should pay for admission or supplies?

Joint custody parents should discuss a monthly budget within their means to cover extra curricular activities for their children. Decisions not specifically addressed in the divorce decree should be made by the parents and presented to the child as a united front.

Which parent should provide transportation home for our child?

Sometimes schools provide a bus to transport children home who participate in after school clubs, however, this varies from community to community. Transportation should be provided by the parent who is able to do so or shared equally, depending upon whose home the child is going to after school. This may be very complicated to arrange. Creative ideas such as carpools, relatives and friends may need to be tapped into so your child can participate in a self esteem building activity.

What if parents disagree on after school participation in clubs?

Joint custody divorced parents as well as married parents often disagree on their child's participation in activities. Discussion and compromise should be reached out of the earshot of your child. Your child's primary physician, therapist or Guidance Counselor can help you to determine if after school activities may help your child improve self esteem.

What does the school require for our child to participate in sports?

A physical exam and release from your child's physician or local health clinic is generally a requirement for participation in school sponsored sports activities.

How can parents manage prom and homecoming?
Which parent pays the expenses for prom and homecoming?

Prom and Homecoming are two very expensive voluntary events which your child has the opportunity to participate in. Each community has developed a standard which may or may not be in line with the values of your family. A frank discussion with your child about your rules of their participation as well as finances should occur early on. Avoid succumbing to community pressure. You may find there are other parents who agree with you, despite your child exclaiming that "everyone" is spending extravagant sums of money on their prom. Discuss with your ex ahead of time a compromise of how much each parent will contribute and how much your child is expected to contribute.

What is our child's responsibility regarding participation in after school clubs?

Your child is responsible to bring home any notices regarding after school clubs and show them to both parents. Your child is responsible to obtain all the information and details of any club they wish to participate in. Your child is responsible to maintain their grades to the best of their ability while participating in after school clubs.

How can we help our child be responsible and enjoy these opportunities?

Children develop and enhance a positive sense of self esteem when participating in a club which addresses their interests and strengths. Your encouragement for their participation will promote an interest, especially in children who are ambivalent. Reminders, support and assistance in maintaining grades will be more effective than threats.

"Aaron's After School Activity Aftershock – Oops!"

Aaron joined the Key Club at his high school, which provided opportunities for community service and leadership. Aaron discovered that if he helped others, he didn't feel sorry for himself. After a full year of feeling sorry for himself after his parents divorced, Aaron was ready to move on with life. He was relieved that he got to spend time with both his parents and even though they did not get along with each other, he respected both of their opinions. It was his time to make a life for himself and stop worrying about the divorce. After all, both his parents seemed to move on and his two younger sisters seemed to be adjusting fine going to dance class and play dates all week and every weekend. All Aaron needed was transportation home after school on Wednesdays and to his community service projects on Saturdays. Once a month he was helping at a local soup kitchen, once a month he was visiting seniors at a nursing home, and once a month he helped disabled children play sports. Aaron's mom explained that Wednesdays conflicted with his sister's dance class and sometimes she could drive him on Saturdays, depending upon the family schedule. His dad wasn't sure about Saturdays either, but would try to arrange to pick him up from school on Wednesdays. Aaron knew he could not commit himself to these projects if he did not have transportation lined up so he explained the problem to the sponsoring teacher. Mr. Wallace understood and recommended that Aaron research public transportation for the weekends and try to arrange a carpool for Wednesdays. He found another boy in the club whose mom offered to drive Aaron home on Wednesdays, but Aaron felt awkward accepting the ride when he wasn't able to reciprocate. The other mom said not to worry, Aaron was doing something good for the community and that was his way of paying it forward. The Saturday schedule was more difficult, however. There was no public transportation near his home and each week Aaron worried about finding the right time to ask his parents for rides. His mother told him to check with his dad and his dad told him that he wasn't sure yet. How could Aaron commit to these projects without being consistent, he wondered. Maybe he should just forget the whole thing and stay home. His parents didn't really care about him as much as his sisters anyway. They didn't understand how important this was to him and didn't even ask him about his projects. Being elected to President of Key Club didn't interest them as much as his sisters' dance recitals. He should probably just drop out and forget the whole thing, Aaron decided.

"Andrea's After School Activity Aces- WOW!"

Andrea continued to earn all A's in fifth grade, even after her parents divorced three years ago. Her parents and her teachers were beginning to worry about Andrea and she was being described as withdrawn. Andrea knew that it meant that she was spending more time alone and was very quiet. She was quiet at school, she was quiet at home with her mom and she was quiet when visiting her dad during their every other weekend visit. Her parents brought her to see a therapist, but she was quiet in the therapist's office as well. So what if she was quiet and withdrawn, Andrea wondered. She got good grades, followed all school rules and did her chores at home, so Andrea didn't understand what the problem was. Her best friend, Susan was the only one who understood. And she promised not to tell anyone the secret. Andrea missed having her parents married and living together. Andrea didn't dare tell them because both her mom and dad were each engaged to other people, both getting married some time soon. She liked her new step parents and was happy to see both her mom and dad happy again, but still wished for her old life back with both of them together as a family. Andrea felt guilty and selfish for wanting this and didn't dare tell anyone except Susan. Susan just listened and told her that everything would get better soon. Susan knew that it would never get all better, but since her own parents were divorced she knew what it was like to want to have your parents back together again. Susan loved her new step parents and no longer felt sad about her parents divorce, at least almost never. All Andrea wanted to do was stay in her room and draw. She drew still lives of fruit and nature. Nature didn't divorce. Andrea's teacher nominated Andrea for an advanced art club at her school being run by the art teacher. Only six students were accepted due to the cost of materials and room size, but mostly because the art teacher wanted to foster talent by giving extra attention to promising young artists. Andrea wanted to go but was worried that Susan would not be there. It was Susan who convinced her to join the club and her mother and father alternated picking her up from school on Tuesday afternoons. Andrea's artwork was displayed in the school hallways, the principal's office and in the superintendent's office at the school board building!! Soon, students and teachers were approaching Andrea in the hallway complimenting her artwork. She smiled more and talked more to others. Andrea didn't feel sad as often about her parents divorce and didn't spend as much time in her room alone anymore. She was still best friends with Susan, who was right after all; things did get better.

Important points to remember about your child's after school activities

Your child may look forward to an after school club as the highlight of their week, with an opportunity to have fun with their friends and develop a skill. These structured activities provide a tremendous benefit to their developing social and leadership skills as well as

Part III

Significant Times for Parents to Be at Your Child's School

Chapter Twenty-Three

Registration: Riddles or Reassurances

What forms do I need to complete for our child's school registration?
What documents should I bring with me when registering my child for school?

There are a number of required forms and documents in the registration process for a new school. The school Registrar will inform you of what is needed. Generally, proof of residence, birth certificate, immunization records, recent physical exam and report card from previous school is required. You will also need to complete forms indicating who your child lives with, who is permitted to remove your child from school, emergency contact phone numbers, income information if applying for the federal free lunch program, and any important medical information regarding your child.

Who is legally permitted to register my child for school?

While it varies in each school district and state, it is generally required that the child's legal guardian register the student for school. There are exceptions for extenuating circumstances which require notarized documents; check with the registrar at your child's new school for further information.

Who's names should I provide for permission to release my child from school?

If your child is sick or there is an emergency, it is important that the school be able to reach you. However, in the event that you are not able to be reached, or unable to go to the school, you will be requested to provide emergency contact names and numbers. Step parents, relatives, neighbors or any trusted friends can be added to this list. Schools will not release your child to an individual not named on your emergency form. Picture ID is being required at many schools at this time for those named on the list.

What important health information does the school need about our child?

The school needs to be aware of any medication being taken by your child, any history of medical problems, allergies or conditions that your child is currently being treated for. The school must keep this information confidential; however it is important for them to be aware of your child's medical conditions for the best interest of your child.

Who will the school call if there is an emergency with our child?

If there is an emergency with your child, the school will attempt to reach you at the contact numbers you have provided. They will then go down the list to the other emergency contact individuals you provided at registration. It is imperative that you keep these contact numbers and names updated in case of an emergency. In the case of life threatening emergencies, 911 will be contacted before taking the time to call you.

Should I give my partner or my ex's partner permission to release my child?

If your partner and your ex's partner are responsible caretakers for your child, giving them permission to release your child from school in the event you are unable to would be of assistance to you and reassuring to your child.

Who is permitted to take my child home from school in the middle of the day?

Any individuals you list on the form provided to you for that purpose are permitted to release your child from school. Many schools are now requiring picture identification from any adult removing a child from school. Avoid involving the school in investigating legal custody by making sure to list your child's joint custody parent on this form if that parent is involved in your child's school career.

What is the federal free and reduced lunch form?

The federal government provides free and reduced cost lunches for students whose family income falls within the poverty level. You will be required to complete an application and may be required to provide documentation of income level.

What if our child does not have medical insurance?

Your child is not required to have medical insurance to attend school. The school can give you information about programs for low cost medical insurance for students, depending upon the community you reside in.

What immunizations are required for our child to attend school?
What if we did not immunize our child for religious or medical reasons?

You child's doctor's office will have a list of the required immunizations for the grade level your child is attending. Doctor's offices are accustomed to providing documentation to schools and have the most up to date requirement which vary from state to state. An exemption is offered for parents who do not wish to immunize their children for religious or medical reasons.

What if our child goes to a private school – who is responsible for the tuition?

Joint custody divorced parents should have financial arrangements agreed upon before registering their child in a private school which charges tuition. The billing offices do not wish to become involved in financial disputes between parents and do not want to be reading through court orders. At the time of registration, the parent or parents who will be responsible for the tuition and other fees will be required to sign a contract regarding payment.

What is our child's responsibility in the registration process?

Your child is responsible to attend the school with you while you are providing information and assist with information as needed. It is important for your child to be aware of the information you are providing to the school and understand procedures for being picked up from school by someone other than yourself.

What steps can we take to ensure a smooth registration process?

In order to ensure a smooth registration process, it is best to contact the school's registrar ahead of time and inquire as to the exact information and documents you will be required to provide at the time of registration. Be prepared to spend time completing the process without feeling rushed or stressed due to time.

"Rena's Registration Riddle – Oops!"

At the last minute, Rena's mom got called into work on the day she was scheduled off and was going to register Rena at her new school. After the divorce, Rena's mother could not afford to turn down any overtime, as she was barely making the monthly bills, even with the child support from Rena's father. She resented that she had to take care of all the appointments for Rena and her father got to do all the fun things with her. Well tomorrow Rena's dad was going to honor his obligation as a joint custody parent; Rena's mom insisted that he take off from work and take Rena to register her at her new school. She asked him, actually told him in front of Rena when he was dropping her off after their weekend visit. She knew he had to say yes in front of his daughter so she purposely did it that way. Rena was so excited about her new school and was happy that her dad was taking her to register. Rena's dad picked her up Monday morning on time, to her mom's surprise, and she couldn't help making a snide comment about his being on time for once. But when they got to the school, the registrar was not available to help them for almost an hour. It was hard for Rena's dad to entertain an eight year old in a school office, but Rena was well behaved. The next hour, her dad spent completing forms, much of which he did not have the proper information for. He was sure that Rena's mom purposely did not provide him with the documents needed – birth certificate, immunization record, proof of residence. He did the best that he could and explained that Rena's mother would come back with the rest. Rena was disappointed that she could not attend school that day and her father had to arrange for a babysitter so he could get to his job. Since Rena's mother put him in a difficult position, he would make sure she knew what it felt like so he did not explain the forms needed, just dropped off the packet and told Rena's mom to be at the school the next day. Rena's mom arrived early and again, Rena had to patiently wait until the registrar was available and her mom added more information to the forms. But Rena could still not begin school because her mom did not bring her birth certificate. She would have to get it from the safety deposit box in the bank which she could have done yesterday had Rena's father told her about it ahead of time. Rena's mom was so busy being angry at Rena's dad, that she didn't notice Rena's disappointment at not being able to begin her new school for the two days she was looking forward to. Rena hoped she could begin tomorrow.

"Roland's Registration Reassurance – WOW!"

Roland's mother was overwhelmed by all the forms and documents she needed to complete in order to enroll her son in Kindergarten. She just got finished with the paperwork from the divorce, move and new job, but this school registration paperwork was as much as all three! She was glad that she called the school and picked up the forms ahead of time and could take her time completing them. Roland needed to get a physical and his doctor's office would need to complete a medical form and an immunization form. There was the emergency form, health form, insurance form, free lunch form, acknowledgement of school policy and procedure form, medication form, bus form and an invitation to join the PTA and be a volunteer! She needed to provide two proofs of residence, Roland's birth certificate, and social security number. Roland's mom was trying to adjust to her new life as a divorced woman and single mom. At least her ex had joint custody and shared in the decision making. They selected this school together and Roland's mom found an apartment in the school district. Roland's dad reminded his mom to put all his contact numbers on the emergency forms and made it clear he intended to take an important role in Roland's life which included his school. His mother really didn't want to have as much contact with his father as joint parenting would involve, but she knew it would be best for Roland to have both his parents involved in important decision in raising him. She wasn't so sure how this would work out in the future years, but for now, she wanted to get through the registration so Roland could have a smooth beginning at school.

---

*Important points to remember about registering our child for school

It is only necessary for one parent to officially register their child for school; ideally it would be in the best interest of both joint custody parents to be there at registration. Both parents can learn of the school's policies and procedures firsthand and understand legal requirements, complete emergency forms and show support to your child.

Chapter Twenty-Four

Beginning a New School: Sitcom or Success

What can we expect for our child's first day at a new school?

The first day your child attends a new school is both anxiety producing and exciting for your child. It can be an overwhelming experience for some children and they will need a lot of reassurance.

How can we help prepare our child for a new school?

Parents can request to arrange a tour of the new school with their child and meet their new teacher(s) ahead of time, depending upon the grade level and policy of the school. Maintaining a positive, hopeful and upbeat attitude about the new school and change in general will go a long way to reduce your child's fears.

What if our child is beginning the new school in the middle of the term?

Many students see an opportunity to make an additional friend when a new student enters a classroom. Schools often assign a peer to orient new students with a tour of the school and friendly welcome.

What policies and procedures should we become familiar with?
What schedules and lists should we request?

Make sure that both joint custody parents receive a copy of the school's discipline policy as well as school handbook, websites, hotlines, school schedule, report card dates, bus schedule, cafeteria menu, parent organizations, attendance policy and emergency policies.

Should both parents be there for our child's first day at a new school?

If it is possible for both joint custody parents to be at their child's school for their first day at a new school, your child might feel reassured, depending upon their age. Cooperating parents can arrange to have one parent take the child to school and the other parent pick the child up for their first day.

How can we help our child make new friends?

You can help your child make new friends by attending any parent meetings and making an effort to meet the parents of your child's classmates. Volunteering to chaperone a field trip or assist in the classroom will also help introduce you to other parents. You can also encourage your middle and high school children to join after school clubs and organizations.

How can we meet the teacher, principal, counselor and other school staff?

Specific meeting times are set aside for parents to meet with the principal, school counselor and other support staff. Attendance at Open House, PTA and membership in school wide committees will also give you a further opportunity to get to know the school staff. If you are registering your child in mid year, do not hesitate to request to be introduced to the principal, grade level administrator, Guidance Counselor and any other support staff who may be available at the time your are registering.

What is our child's responsibility in beginning a new school?

Your child is responsible to maintain a positive and hopeful attitude, follow all class and school rules and bring home all school papers and schoolwork to show both joint custody divorced parents.

How can we help our child make a smooth transition to a new school?

Joint custody divorced parents may be forced to enroll their children in a new school due to a move necessitated by the divorce. Attending a new school may be just one of the many changes your child is experiencing due to the divorce. Maintain a positive and hopeful attitude toward change. Be aware of their anxiety and provide reassurance during this transition time.

"Saul's New School Sitcom – Oops!"

Saul thought he was the only child in the world to have his parents divorced, his mom go back to work, move to a new home and go to a new school. Well, perhaps not the only child in the world, but certainly the only one in his class. Saul thought he might be able to adjust to the divorce since he continued to see his dad every Wednesday evening and every other weekend. His dad also came to all his baseball games and called him every evening. Sometimes they even emailed each other! That part was okay so far, but Saul didn't like to have his mom going back to work. That meant he had to go to aftercare at school instead of coming home each day. His mom explained that now that she was divorced, she had to get a job to pay the bills, but she would still help him with his homework and make dinner for him when they got home. Saul didn't care about homework or dinner, he wanted to go out and play with his friends in the neighborhood after school. Saul did manage to adjust to aftercare where he got to complete most of his homework and play with some new friends so it was okay after all. But then Saul's mom explained that they had to move to a smaller apartment since their house was too expensive. And the worst part was that Saul would be attending a new school in the next town where he didn't have one single friend! Fourth grade, parents divorced, new after care, new home, new school – it was now feeling too much for Saul. He usually had no problem making new friends but with his parents divorced, he was not up to any more changes and dreaded the new school. He did wonder if they had a nice gym and playground and if the boys in his new neighborhood played baseball. Saul wondered if he would be taking the bus, who his teacher would be, and if the other students in his new class were friendly. His dad gave him a new baseball cap to wear at his new school, but the first thing the teacher did when she met him was to tell him to remove it! No caps allowed in school. Saul was also told that jeans were not allowed, only khaki pants and solid shirts. Saul didn't know about the school dress policy and here he was in the first day in class with jeans and a cool baseball jersey. He couldn't wait for the day to be over, as he had the wrong school supplies with him, no reading log and had trouble following the class routine. Saul never had trouble in school before so this was new to him. Two other boys tried to be friends with Saul during lunch and recess but Saul was not interested in making new friends at that moment. All he could think about was his parents getting back together, moving back to his new house and going back to his old school.

"Suzanne's New School Success – WOW!"

Suzanne's dad and mom told her they needed to talk with her together. The last time they talked with her together was to tell her that they would be getting a divorce. That was two years ago and they were sad to tell Suzanne about their plans, but have kept their promise to both spend time with her and keep her at the same home and same school. Now they were explaining to Suzanne that they needed to make changes. The house was too expensive to keep up and Suzanne and her mother would need to move. They were going to move into a smaller townhouse in another town and Suzanne would still get to spend time with her dad every week. Even though she was in ninth grade and fourteen years old, Suzanne still liked spending time with him. Now her parents were explaining that she would be able to complete the ninth grade at her school but would move at the end of the school year and begin tenth grade in a new school. Suzanne tried to remain calm but the thought of leaving her friends and going to a school where she knew no one made her feel very anxious and scared. Suzanne's dad could read her mind and said he knew that leaving her friends would be very difficult. Suzanne's mom had a plan. If Suzanne could work as a volunteer camp counselor at the community center in their new town this summer, she could make new friends who would be attending her high school. Suzanne's mother also showed her information on the swim team sponsored by the community center. Suzanne thought that maybe that was a good idea since she loved swimming, but said that she needed time to think about it. The next week, Suzanne's mom asked her if she would like to take a tour of the new school. Suzanne wasn't sure that she was ready to think about it but agreed to go anyway. The kids at the new school looked just like the kids at Suzanne's school. She was even allowed to attend one of the classes and several of the girls talked to her and gave her a tour of the school. They asked her if she was interested in joining any after school clubs and said they looked forward to seeing her at school next year. Suzanne felt that she had made two new friends already! Maybe she could introduce them to her old friends, and maybe it would be fun to join the swim team and work at the summer camp after all.

Important points to remember about our child's new school

Schools are open to suggestions. If you have an idea that would help make your child's transition to a new school smoother, do not hesitate to make a recommendation to the school. For some children, the thought of attending a new school is the most anxiety producing event in their life. Be sensitive to your child's feelings about a new school, friends and changes in general. Consider creative ways to support new friendships as this will be the most crucial component in your child's transition to a new school.

Chapter Twenty-Five

Open House/Parent Night: Horrors or Hoorays

*What is Open House at school?

Open House at your child's school is a scheduled evening for parents to visit the school and meet their child's teacher(s). It is traditionally held during the first month of school.

*What is the purpose of an Open House?

The purpose of Open House is for parents and teachers to meet in person, and for parents to see their child's classroom or classrooms and get an overview of curriculum and procedures at school.

*Which parent should attend our child's school Open House?

Both joint custody parents should attend their child's open house at school if at all possible.

*Can I bring my partner? Should my ex bring their partner?

If your partner or your ex's partner are a part of your child's school life, such as helping with homework and projects then it would be helpful for them to attend as well.

*Do we bring our child to Open House? What about siblings?

Open House is generally just for parents and children are not invited or expected to attend. Check with your child's school about their policy regarding children attending Open House. Make every opportunity to arrange for a babysitter for younger children so that you may focus your attention on the Open House.

Can we spend a moment with the teacher talking about our child?

Open House is designed for parents to meet the teacher and for the teacher to explain to parents what material is covered in the curriculum and information about the class policies. Your child's teacher might make a positive comment about your child when meeting you; however, this is not an opportunity to discuss your child's particular performance.

What are some important questions to ask at Open House?

Teachers want to be sure that parents understand their expectations for school supplies, class work, homework, studying, research, note taking, tests, quizzes, projects, grading policy, discipline policy, make-up work policy and any other classroom procedures. If you have questions about curriculum or any of the above, teachers wish to explain this further to you and the other parents in attendance so that you may support your child to do their best in the teacher's class.

What is our child's responsibility regarding their school Open House?

Your child is responsible to bring home any notices which invite you to open house and share with both joint custody parents. Your child may also be requested to complete a schedule for you to follow for middle and high school, since many open houses involve the parents changing classes as their children do.

How can we help ensure a successful Open House experience?

You can assure a smooth Open House experience by being gracious when meeting your child's teacher, taking notes, asking questions and sharing the information with your ex if they are unable to attend.

"Hazel's Open House Horror – Oops!"

Hazel was excited about her mother meeting her fourth grade teacher, Mrs. Newman, the nicest teacher she had so far. On the night of Open House, Hazel's grandmother was babysitting for her since only parents were invited. Hazel drew a picture for her mother and wrote her a note that day in school, the last assignment for the day before dismissal. She also wrote a note for her dad, who said he would try to attend the Open House at Hazel's school. Hazel's parents had been divorced for just over a year and her dad and mom still did not get along. Hazel's mom made it clear to Hazel that she did not want to see or speak to her dad which made it awkward when Hazel's dad picked her up for visits several times a week. He stayed in the car waiting for Hazel to come out. The few times he did come in, Hazel's mother made nasty comments about his new car, new girlfriend or child support payments being behind. Hazel's mom acknowledged to Hazel that she was angry with Hazel's dad and decided to just not be in the same room with him. Of course, Hazel knew that Open House was an exception. When she told her mom that her dad might be attending the Open House, Hazel's heart fell at her mother's response: "Well, if he is going, then I will not!" Hazel tried to reason with her and even told her about the picture and letter which was supposed to be a surprise, but her mother's mind was made up. She would not allow herself to be in the same room with Hazel's dad and that was final. Hazel wished she did not tell her mom about her dad possibly going, but she agreed to keep no secrets from either parent when they divorced. Perhaps it was better that her mom knew ahead of time anyway, she might have just walked out and made an embarrassing scene if she were at the Open House and Hazel's dad showed up surprising her. It turned out that her dad was not able to be at the Open House after all, his meeting at work ran overtime. The next day at school when Hazel's teacher asked why neither of her parents were able to be at Open House, Hazel did not know what to say. She wondered if she should tell Mrs. Newman about how much her mom hated her dad and wouldn't be in the same room with him. Even if Mrs. Newman did understand, she might think Hazel's mom was not very nice or that her father was not a nice person. Mrs. Newman might then think if Hazel's parents weren't very nice then maybe Hazel was not a very nice girl either.

"Herman's Open House Hooray – WOW!"

Herman asked his fifth grade teacher if it was okay for his parents to both attend Open House even if they were divorced. Of course they were both welcome to attend, Herman's teacher assured him. Herman did not know just how to ask the teacher his next question of whether it was okay for his dad to bring his partner. Herman's dad's partner was a man. Herman's mom got along fine with her ex husband and his partner which made it easy for Herman to accept and like his dad's partner as well. Jim, his dad's partner, was better in science and math than either of his parents and often helped Herman with his homework. Herman really wanted Jim to attend the Open House but did not know if his teacher would understand or approve. He did not even know how to ask. Fortunately, Herman's teacher made an announcement that there was enough room for all parents to attend and bring along any other adult friends or family members who wanted to learn about the school and classroom. She explained that anyone who helped with homework and projects would benefit from attending the Open House. Herman knew that included Jim as well and was happy that he did not have to explain to his teacher. His best friend, Joseph knew about Herman's dad's partner Jim, because he visited Herman at his dad's house one weekend. Herman's dad spoke privately with Joseph's mom who already knew of the situation from Herman's mom. Joseph and his mom didn't care and were happy that Jim was able to help Joseph study for his math test. As it turned out, Herman's teacher never asked who Jim was. He was sitting with both Herman's mom and dad and was introduced as an important person in Herman's life. It was a good thing he did attend the Open House, because the teacher explained the new math unit the class would be studying the next week and it was very difficult. Jim helped Herman get a head start on understanding the math concepts. Joseph wanted to come to Herman's dad's house to have Jim help him when he got a D on the first math test. Herman wasn't sure how he would introduce Jim to his other friends and teachers in the following years, but was relieved to know it was okay for the rest of fifth grade. Maybe he didn't need to worry about what other people thought of the situation after all. If his mom was fine with it, and he was fine with it, then maybe it didn't matter anyway what people in the future might think.

*What are some important points to remember about Open House at school?

Remember to consider the best interest of your child when attending their school Open House. Your child will benefit from your ex's attendance, even if it is difficult for you. Make every effort to attend this one time yearly event so that you can be the best support possible for your child's successful school year.

Chapter Twenty-Six

Parent/Teacher Conferences: Circus or Consensus

What is the purpose of a parent teacher conference?
Parent teacher conferences are held for several different purposes: sharing with the parents the academic and social progress of their child, gathering information and providing suggestions to assist the child, and developing strategies to overcome barriers to success and happiness in school for the child.

Who is responsible for scheduling the conference?
How often are parent teacher conferences held?
Elementary school teachers often schedule conferences twice yearly with all parents as a routine. Often in Middle and High Schools, conferences are only scheduled if requested by parent or teacher if there is a problem to address. This varies between districts therefore it is best to check with your child's school and teacher about the conference policy.

How long will the conference last?
Teachers are generally on a tight schedule for conferences which last for an average of about thirty minutes.

Should both divorced parents attend the conference together?
Should either parent bring their partner?
It is helpful for the teacher to present information regarding your child's progress once to both joint custody divorced parents rather than repeat it twice at two different conferences. If your partner and your ex's partner are involved in your child's education, it is helpful for them to attend as well in order to hear the information first hand.

139

Should our child attend the conference? How about siblings?

If there is information being shared that the child is not aware of, or would be detrimental for the child to learn of, then do not include your child. Children as young as Kindergarten can benefit from attending at least part of a parent teacher conference to hear how they are progressing and help develop plans for improvement. Siblings are generally not appropriate to bring to a conference.

Do I have to take time off from work to attend our child's conference?

Most schools schedule conferences during the school hours, during the teacher planning time before or after classroom instruction. Teacher's are generally not given paid time for evening conferences with parents.

How can we prepare for a parent teacher conference?

You can prepare for the parent teacher conference by developing a list of your child's strengths, interests, challenges and your questions ahead of time. Give some consideration to some ideas to help improve specific areas your child is struggling with.

Can we just talk to the teacher(s) on the telephone or via email?

Inquire with your child's school and their teacher as to the district's policy regarding telephone and email conferences. It is beneficial to meet with the teacher face to face at least once during the school year and follow up if needed with telephone or email.

What is our child's responsibility regarding parent teacher conferences?

Your child is responsible to bring home any notes from the teacher requesting a conference and return notes to the teacher from parents. Your child is responsible to participate in the conference for the portion they are requested to attend and provide honest appraisal of their progress along with any ideas for improvement if needed.

How can we ensure a productive parent teacher conference?

It is important to be on time, be courteous, and be prepared. If there is underlying hostility between you and your ex, avoid bringing it into

140

the parent teacher conference. Be gracious by sitting in the same room with your ex, even if it is difficult for you to do.

"Caleb's Parent Teacher Conference Circus – Oops!"

Caleb's teacher wanted him to sit in at the parent teacher conference with his mother so he did. It was the first time he was invited to a conference so he was nervous and curious as to what to expect. Caleb wished he could crawl under the table and become invisible once he found out how the conference was going to be. Caleb heard his mother and teacher taking turns describing all the rules he breaks at home and in school, everything he forgets and even his hygiene. Fifth grade boys forget to do their homework sometimes and Caleb thought that was normal. According to his mother and teacher, he sounded like the worst boy in the world! Neither mentioned the home run he hit in little league last week or the math homework he handed in and got all the answers correct yesterday! Just when he thought it couldn't get any worse, Caleb's mother brought up Caleb's dad and how irresponsible he was as a father. Caleb knew his dad could not be at the conference because he had to work and didn't think it was fair that his mother was saying bad things about him to his teacher. Caleb wanted to defend his father but didn't dare say anything. He didn't want to make it get even worse. Anytime he tried to defend his father since the divorce, his mother would say that his father didn't deserve Caleb's love. He hated hearing her say that and certainly didn't want to hear his mother say that in front of his teacher so he just kept quiet. And then it was over. Finally. Caleb saw the clock and was surprised that only thirty minutes had passed – it seemed like hours.

"Christine's Parent Teacher Conference Consensus - WOW!"

Christine's teacher apologized for having only small student chairs for Christine's entire set of parents to sit at during their conference. Christine thought her mom, step dad, dad and step mom looked funny sitting in the student chairs, as if they were pretending to be students. It was hard to be nervous at the conference when Christine thought about how funny the adults looked in small chairs. Everyone was smiling even though they were talking about a problem. Christine did not understand her math homework and would get upset and frustrated. All of her parents wanted some ideas on how to help her as they all got frustrated too. Christine's teacher explained the math in class but Christine would forget it by the time she was home. Everyone was tired of the arguing in trying to get Christine to try to do better with her math homework. Christine's teacher explained that math was a hard subject and many of her third grade students over the years had difficulty with it. That made Christine feel a little better. Christine's teacher recommended some fun games and websites which would help Christine remember her math concepts. She even showed her parents how she taught math. Then she asked where and when Christine does her math homework. At her mom's house where she lived every other week, she did her homework after dinner. At her dad's house, she did her homework in the morning before school. Christine's teacher recommended doing math homework as soon as she gets home so the lesson is fresh in her mind. All four parents agreed to that. Christine's teacher also recommended no TV, radio or any distractions while doing homework. Her parents listened to other ideas and each praised Christine's wonderful strengths. Christine was no longer nervous and thought that she was lucky to have four parents who cared about her. Maybe she would be able to try harder on her homework each night and not give up so quickly if it is difficult.

---

*Important points to remember about parent teacher conferences

Teachers are accustomed to working with children and can sometimes feel uncomfortable with parents, especially when providing information regarding lack of academic progress, motivation or social skills. Do your best to work as a team to overcome any problems your child is having – teachers are truly working towards the best interests of your child.

Chapter Twenty-Seven

Special Education Program: Erosion or Easy

What is the Special Education Program?

The Special Education Program is the school's response to legal requirements that protect discrimination of individuals with disabilities. IDEA and 504 are two of these laws which not only prevent discrimination but entitle all students to meaningful access to and the potential to benefit from their education. The name used to describe this program may be different your home state.

Does this mean our child is handicapped?

If your child qualifies for the special education program, it means that they need accommodations beyond what the average child will need to learn.

What is an Individual Educational Plan (IEP)?

An IEP is a written document which describes the educational category which your child qualifies for accommodations and lists the accommodations that will be provided to your child. The IEP will also list educational or behavioral goals and timelines for meeting these goals as well as who will be responsible for monitoring these accommodations and goals. An example would be a daily home note from the teacher, extra time to complete tests or the use of a computer for note taking. A different name may be used in your state to describe this written plan.

Should both parents attend the IEP staffing? Should our child attend?

It would be an advantage for both joint custody divorced parents to attend the IEP staffing in order to understand your child's current academic abilities and progress firsthand and have input towards goals and plans to meet goals.

Should I bring my partner? Should my ex bring their partner?

If your partner and your ex's partner are involved in your child's education, then it would be an advantage for them and for your child to have them attend the IEP Staffing.

How often are these meetings held?

IEP Staffings are held annually, with additional meetings if needed between the yearly ones. Parents can request an additional meeting, called a Review.

Is this important enough for us to take off from work to attend?

It is important for parents to attend annual staffings in order to help develop annual goals.

What are our legal rights as parents regarding our child's education and the Special Education Program?

The contact person at your school who is in charge of coordinating the Special Education Program for your child will provide you with a booklet which lists your legal rights as parents. You will be asked to sign a document indicating that you received this information. Make sure to ask questions if you are unclear of your rights.

What are all of these forms we are being asked to sign?

The Special Education Program is monitored by the federal government since they are providing funding for services. Auditors will monitor these documents in your child's file to ensure that all services being provided are appropriate and your child's legal rights to an education are being met.

How is it determined if our child is eligible for special services?

A lengthy and detailed evaluation of your child's learning styles and educational needs will be conducted by the school which includes observations, psycho educational testing, and checklists completed by the teacher and the parents.

Who is on the team that decides how to best educate our child?

The team consists of the child's parent(s), teachers(s), a Special Education representative, and any other school support person who attends the meeting such as School Psychologist, Behavior Specialist, Reading Specialist, Speech Therapist and Guidance Counselor. You are also permitted to bring a Parent Advocate or any support person you wish to attend with you.

What if we disagree with the school's assessment of our child's needs?
What if my ex and I disagree with each other as to our child's special needs?

Everyone's opinions will be heard and recorded. It is not unusual for there to be a difference of opinion between parents or professionals when observing a child's learning experience since children vary their level of participation and cooperation in different settings. All opinions will be considered and team decisions will be made.

Can the school suggest or require parent to give their child medication?

The decision to take medication is a medical decision which is made between the parents and your child's physician. The school is not qualified to advise you on this matter, nor can they request or require that you give your child medication.

Can the school force us to place our child in a special program?

Parent consent is needed to place a child in a special program; however, the school can appeal a parent's decision, according to very specific federal regulations. During the appeal process, your child cannot be placed in a special program without your consent.

What is our child's responsibility regarding the Special Education Program?

It is your child's responsibility to bring home forms that tell you about the annual IEP staffings (meetings), attend part of the meeting if requested and participate by providing information about their educational experience.

*How can we make the Special Education process the most effective for our child?

Carefully read through the information provided to you by the school about the Special Education Program, ask questions, provide input as to your impressions of your child's learning style, and work with the team to develop plans to help your child learn best.

"Esther's Special Education Erosion – Oops!"

Esther wondered what the letter SLD meant on the folder with her name on it that she saw on her teacher's desk. Specific Learning Disability was the answer she was given but Esther didn't know what that had to do with her. Esther was not in a wheelchair so how could she be disabled? Esther asked her mother and her mother could not explain it to her. Esther's mother knew that her daughter, now in sixth grade was receiving extra help in math each year in school since second grade. That was the time Esther's parents were going through with a divorce and Esther kept forgetting to bring home some notices about meetings at school. Her mother would not have been able to attend anyway since she was working overtime to pay bills once she became single. When the school finally sent the papers by mail, Esther's mother didn't understand them but signed as requested since it was explained to her that her daughter would be getting extra help in math. Esther began going to a different teacher several times a week for math help and called it Resource Room. Esther's mother was glad that it helped, but she kept getting notices home each year for her signature. A booklet containing "Procedural Safeguards" also came in the mail and Esther's mother was asked to sign that she received it. As long as Esther was getting the help she needed in math, Esther's mother felt that it was okay to skip the meetings. She didn't bother to explain the extra help in math to Esther's father and he didn't ask. When Esther asked her father what SLD meant and how the school could think she was disabled, he could not answer her either. Esther began to wonder if there was something wrong with her. She no longer wanted to go to Resource Room for extra help in math. When Esther's report card grade dropped to a D in math, Esther's mother was asked to come in for a conference. She didn't think that there was anything she could do to help since she was not good in math, so she didn't go. Esther's father did not know of the conference as Esther's mother didn't tell him. He never even went to Esther' school so she didn't think he would be interested. Esther wanted to get help in math but didn't want to go back to Resource Room if that meant she was handicapped!

"Ephraim's Special Education Easy – WOW!"

Ephraim tried his best but still could not read the simple books in big letters and pictures in his first grade class. His parents thought that maybe he was upset about their divorce and just could not concentrate but they became increasingly more worried about Ephraim. Even though they were divorced, Ephraim's parents scheduled a parent teacher conference and attended together. They explained to Ephraim's teacher that they had joint custody and gave the teacher a copy of the visitation schedule. Ephraim lived with his mom most of the school week but spent every Thursday evening at his dad. He stayed at his dad's overnight and his dad took him to school every Friday morning. Ephraim's teacher explained that she was requesting further testing on Ephraim's reading ability and asked his parents to complete several questionnaires about Ephraim's life at home. His parents worked on the questionnaire together and then met with the reading specialist at school. She explained that after a screening, she would refer Ephraim to the Special Education Program for further testing. Later that school year, Ephraim's parents were again asked to sign further forms giving their permission to have Ephraim evaluated by a School Psychologist. She explained that she would be giving Ephraim more extensive testing to determine his learning style and strengths as well as weaknesses. Ephraim's parents were invited to a "staffing" by the Special Education Program and both parents attended the meeting. At the staffing, the School Psychologist explained that Ephraim had a reading disability and there were certain teaching techniques that would help him learn to read. A trained teacher would provide extra reading instruction using a special program designed to help children like Ephraim. It was explained to Ephraim's parents that there would be a federal program monitoring Ephraim's progress and a special plan called an Individual Education Plan (IEP) would be written with all members of the committee (which included parents, teachers and the Special Education Specialist) designing the plan and signing it. Ephraim's goals would be evaluated each year, with additional meetings if needed. Much to Ephraim's pride and his parents' relief, Ephraim began reading by the end of the first grade. Both his parents followed the teacher's recommendations and read to him nightly, keeping a reading log and gradually having Ephraim take a turn reading to them. He was given stars at school and by his parents at home for his efforts. Ephraim loved getting his stars because he knew that even though it took him longer to learn to read, he was truly a star!

Important points to remember about the Special Education Program for our child

There are many accommodations available for the school to offer your child in order to improve their learning experience. Be observant and aware of how effective these accommodations are in helping your child learn best. Be part of the team to help plan for your child's special needs by attending meetings and offering your opinion and suggestions.

Chapter Twenty-Eight

Awards Assembly: Asteroids or Awesome

*What is an awards assembly?
*What is the purpose of the school's awards assembly?
    An Awards Assembly is a tradition at most schools where an evening or morning is set aside to help foster pride and motivation for students by recognizing their accomplishments publicly. Your child's school holds awards assemblies in order to present awards to honor effort and achievement for as many students as possible.

*When are awards assemblies usually held?
    Awards assemblies are usually held at the end of the school year and can be scheduled in the morning or evening. Some schools hold mid year or monthly awards assemblies.

*How will we know if our child is receiving an award?
    Some schools will notify the parent in advance if their child is receiving an award in order to encourage attendance, however this information is usually kept confidential until the award is presented.

*Should both parents attend the awards assembly?
    If both joint custody divorced parents can attend this event, it would be in your child's best interest to have both parents in the audience when they receive an award.

*Should my partner attend as well? How about my ex's partner?
*Should we invite grandparents and other relatives?
    Your child will be proud to have the attendance and support of any and all family members if they receive an award.

Do we have to sit next to each other?

If joint custody divorced parents are engaged in a friendly relationship, sitting next to or near each other would be a support for your child. If there is a conflictual relationship, this might be stressful for your child and it would be best to sit several rows apart. If divorced joint custody parents are sitting at opposite ends of the audience, it is stressful for your child to alternate their gaze between two sets of parents. Young children might feel a sense of conflicting loyalty in efforts to look at both parents equally.

Should we take off from work to attend an awards assembly?

Having a parent in the audience when receiving an award at school is an important event for your child. If it is at all possible for you to be there, take off from work. If this is not possible, it is important to make sure a family member or close friend is there as your representative.

Can we take photographs?

Make sure to take photographs of your child receiving the award, and later with their teacher or principal with the award. You may wish to take pictures of your child's friends receiving awards as well. By providing a copy to the parents of your child's friends, you have an opportunity to get to know them better and it will be appreciated. It would be a very nice gesture for you to take a picture of your child with your ex. Not only does this enhance your child's sense of comfort with the divorce, but the photo is a good gift from your child to your ex for holidays, birthdays, Mother's Day and Father's Day.

Is this important to our child?

Your child may verbalize disinterest in the awards assembly; however, will most likely feel very proud when being called on to stage to be honored for an accomplishment in front of students and families.

Which parent gets to keep the award?

The award certificate or trophy belongs to your child and should be kept at the home of the parent of their choice. It is important that parents do not attempt to make the child feel guilty to choose where to keep the award, as this would tarnish the joy and pride from receiving the award.

150

What is our child's responsibility regarding awards assemblies at school?

Your child is responsible to notify you of the awards assembly date by bringing home any notices and informing both joint custody divorced parents of the date. Your child is also expected to be respectful during the awards assembly.

How can we make this a happy memorable experience for our child?

You can make the awards assembly a happy, memorable experience for your child by being there and by being exceptionally gracious to your ex spouse and their partner.

"Paul's Awards Assembly Asteroid – Oops!"

Paul was happy to learn that he was receiving the "Most Improved Student" award this month since he worked so hard to improve his behavior and grades in his fifth grade class. His teacher told him that he really deserved it and to invite his parents to the awards ceremony in the evening. Paul invited both his mom and his dad. Even though they had been divorced for almost a year, he felt sure that they would both want to be there for him. Both his parents explained to him that they would both continue to be his parents after the divorce and both still be involved with his life as part of their joint custody agreement. What Paul didn't expect was for his parents to have a fight at the awards ceremony. His dad criticized his mom for not dressing Paul in dress clothes for the ceremony. His mom responded back that if his dad paid his child support on time that she would have been able to afford nice clothes for Paul. Paul thought he looked just fine in the clothes he wore to school every day. He also thought that his classmates' parents would think less of him after hearing his parents argue. Paul's teacher looked surprised and made a point of talking to Paul privately, explaining that it was not his fault that his parents argued in front of others. She explained that sometimes divorced parents have trouble getting along, even if they do have joint custody. She made Paul feel a little better until the next day when one of his classmates told him that his mother heard the whole argument between Paul's parents and wanted to know who Paul thought was right. Paul did not want to side with either parent and didn't want to discuss it. He wondered how many other parents heard the arguing and what they thought of him. Paul decided that his "Most Improved Student" award was a bad memory – one he wanted to quickly forget.

"Penny's Awards Assembly Awesome – WOW!"

Penny was thrilled to learn that she was selected for a scholarship to a music academy this summer, the summer before her senior year of high school. She had been singing at her church and the school choir since she was seven years old, nearly ten years. When she sang, it helped her feel good about herself, her family and the world. Singing helped Penny get through her sad feelings about her parents divorce five years ago and her best friend's death two years ago. Singing made Penny feel at peace and she decided that she would sing her entire life whether or not she could get a job doing it. She could always sing in a church choir and at home. Penny did not have to explain to either her father or her mother how important singing was to her. They both could see it every time they attended her performances and when she sang at home as well. She was so excited to have both her parents attend the end of the year Awards Assembly at school where Melody Music Academy was going to present the scholarship to her. She did not know that her parents had already discussed how important this was to her and made arrangements for her to have a new dress and flowers for the event. Penny saw both her parents sitting next to each other in the audience, exchanging her mom's borrowed camera taking picture of her. After the ceremony, the parents and students were invited to the school gymnasium where pizza and cake was served by the PTA to honor the award recipients. Penny sat at small table with both of her parents and served them proudly. She knew that they were divorced and had been for five years, but was very aware of how they both shared their tremendous pride of her and thought that this might be the happiest day of her life, so far.

*Important points to remember about our child's school awards assembly

Awards are given for academic achievement in various subjects, attendance, citizenship, most improved and other areas. Teachers often make a special attempt to give a student an award if they are in need of improved self esteem. Children generally feel very special receiving an award from their school, especially if a parent is in the audience.

Chapter Twenty-Nine

Recitals/Plays/Concerts/ Sports Games

What types of recitals, concerts, or plays might our child perform in at school?

Schools present recitals, concerts and plays in order to help children learn and to develop self esteem and pride in their school. Parents and family members are invited to attend so children can feel special about their participation and accomplishment. Sports games are played between teams from other local schools; performances are presented by the drama club or individual classes; the band, orchestra and chorus present performances.

How often and when are these performances held?

The number of performances varies between school districts. Band, orchestra and chorus generally hold performances two to three times each school year, celebrating winter holiday season, end of year events and another holiday season somewhere throughout the school year. These events are generally scheduled in the evening in order to accommodate parents and families. Plays are held by individual classes or grades during certain theme units which the entire class or grade participate in. These special events are generally held during the school day in order to have the entire class or grade participate. The drama club may put on plays several times each school year with student participants who have tried out in order to earn each part in the production. Plays are generally performed on the weekends, with several performances from Friday evening through Sunday daytime. Sports games are held almost weekly for several months, depending upon the sport in season at the time. These games are played immediately following the school day.

Is it important for us to attend every performance and game?

If you are able to, it would be a great encouragement for your child to attend every performance and game. Most parents are unable to attend all of them due to their work schedule. It would be wise to coordinate with all family members in order to have at least one representative of your child's family at every event, such as a grandparent, older sibling or favorite aunt.

Should both parents attend?

Each parent should attend every event they possibly can. This is positive encouragement and support for your child.

What about my partner? My ex's partner? Siblings? Grandparents?

If these individuals are a significant part of your child's life, their attendance will be perceived as support and encouragement by your child, thereby helping to raise and maintain a healthy self esteem.

Are there a limited number of guests allowed per student?

That depends upon the school and the activity. Check with your child's teacher for more information. Generally these events are held in the largest room in the school such as the auditorium or cafeteria in order to accommodate as many family members as possible.

Do we have to sit together?

No, it is not necessary for divorced parents to sit together, however, it would be best to sit in rows near each other. By doing this, your child can see both of you within the same view. Otherwise, (s)he has to turn her/his head back and forth to catch a glimpse of both of you. This might sound trivial, however young children feel torn, sometimes needing to look at each parent an equal number of times for fear of picking favorites.

Are we permitted to take pictures? Who should be in the photos?

Taking pictures enhances the excitement and sense of pride for your child. The picture taking however is best done immediately before and directly following the event in order to not disturb the performance. If pictures can be taken very discreetly during the performance or game

155

without disturbing the participants or audience, take some great shots! Usually an announcement will be made regarding the request of courtesy for picture taking. Make sure to take pictures of your child with their friends, teammates and classmates, as well as the entire group of performers. Taking a picture of your child with their coach or teacher is a great ego boost as well. Your child will also enjoy having photo's of themselves with the family members who attended, so make certain to take pictures of your child with your ex and ask someone to take a picture of you and your child together!

Which parent should pay for the uniform or equipment our child needs?

This is something to discuss privately with your ex, long before the need arises so that your child does not get caught in the middle of a disagreement. Often schools have a special fund for those in financial need so that no child is left out due to inability to pay for the uniform or necessary supplies. This is also an appropriate time to ask for help from relatives such as grandparents who often take much joy in paying for special purchases for their grandchildren.

Which parent should take the child out to celebrate after the performance?

This is another private discussion between divorced parents that your child need not be distracted with worry about. It is not necessary, but sometimes customary for the child to celebrate with their family at an ice cream shop before going home directly after the event. Be a sport and offer that honor to your ex. Your child will appreciate the gesture.

What is our child's responsibility regarding school performances and games?

Your child is responsible to bring home notices and inform their parents in a timely manner of the dates of performances and games so that parents may have enough time in advance to arrange for time off from work or child care if needed. Your child is responsible to focus on their best performance on the day of the game or event. Your child is responsible to greet each family member and thank them for attending.

How can we make this an exciting and proud event for our child?

Use your imagination! Prepare a hand made congratulations sign to greet them upon their arrival home, keep the program displayed on the refrigerator or bulletin board at home, take lots of photos and smile during the performance. Do not bring bad manners, a negative attitude or a date to the performance. Treat your ex respectfully, despite any bitter, angry or sad feelings you may have. Show your child that this is about them!

Rachel's Recital Road Show –OOPS!

Rachel was fourteen years old in the ninth grade, her first year of high school. This was her first band concert and she was first chair in the flute section! The three years of practice her mom had to bug her about most of the time really paid off. She was so happy that her father was attending her concert even if her mother hated him after four years of divorce. At least she did not have to listen to them fighting anymore, except when her dad came to the door to pick her up for a visit every other weekend. That's when her mother would bring up late child support payments and make snide remarks about her dad having enough money to buy a new car or new sneakers for himself. Rachel tried to solve that problem on her own by making sure to be ready and run out to the car as soon as he arrived. That was not working too well, however because he was usually late to pick her up. And he was late tonight to her concert. The seats were filling up fast and it looked like they ran out of programs. Maybe her mother took an extra one. Rachel's mother was in the front row with camera ready to roll. Although Rachel appreciated her support, she wished her mother would have more of a life of her own.

Finally her dad arrived, but not alone. Rachel's heart sank when she realized that her father brought a woman with him. It looked like Jennifer, his new girlfriend, a very pretty blond who was fifteen years younger than her father. Rachel couldn't believe that her father brought a date to her first school concert! Rachel found herself worried about her mother's feelings. Just when she was hoping her mother wouldn't see her dad, Rachel missed the instruction from the band director to position their chairs and begin to tune their instruments. Luckily, her best friend Nancy who sat behind her nudged Rachel and helped her refocus.

Nancy had been her best friend since fourth grade but she wouldn't understand how upset Rachel was feeling now; Nancy's parents were happily married and sitting together in the audience three rows behind Rachel's mom. Oh, no! Rachel noticed her mother eyeing her dad with Jennifer and she knew instantly what her mother was thinking – her dad had a new girlfriend who was younger, thinner and prettier than she was. Lately, Rachel's mom was trying to diet but she explained that her hormones were changing and it made it difficult to keep her weight down. Rachel could almost feel the hurt in her mother's heart; after all, they were close like sisters.

Nancy was nudging Rachel again, it was time to begin. What was the first song, the first note, she tried to remember but Rachel kept noticing her father holding hands with Jennifer in the seats they found one row behind her mother! Someone didn't show up for their saved seats and her father was lucky enough to find them. Or unlucky for Rachel's mother, who was starting to turn red with rage. Jennifer was pretty; she almost could hear Nancy's mother whisper so to her own husband. Rachel couldn't actually hear that far away but she was sure she knew what Nancy's mother and everyone was thinking.

Oh no! Rachel missed the first note of the first song of her first concert of her first year in high school. Focus, concentrate, okay, she began playing and remembered how much she learned to love the flute. The beautiful sound Rachel could draw from the instrument helped her forget about how much her mother was depressed about getting old, about being single and about not having enough money. It was the first thing she found to help her stop thinking about her sadness about the divorce and her parents constant fighting. Before she knew it, the first song was over and except for the first note, Rachel played flawlessly! The rest of the concert was great, as long as Rachel did not see her dad and Jennifer holding hands or her mother looking sad and angry. Rachel actually felt proud to have both of her parents there even though they were not sitting together.

After the concert was over, Rachel ran to her dad who had flowers waiting for her. He explained that was why he was late. Rachel loved receiving flowers from her dad, but her joy was tarnished when he told her it was Jennifer's suggestion. Rachel turned around just in time to hear her mother tell Nancy's mother how her father could afford flowers but not pay child support on time! Rachel wanted to tell her mother to stop, but she couldn't give her mother "the look" before one final comment was made about how Rachel's dad never took any of her suggestions when they were married! Rachel had heard it all before. Her mother paid for her concert clothes, drove her to practices in the morning, paid for the flute rental, the extra mouthpieces, and the sheet music. She supported all the fund raisers, even went to all the band parent meetings. According to Rachel's mother, Rachel's father did not deserve to share in the joy and glory of Rachel's band concert. Why couldn't her mother understand that it was Rachel's concert, not her mother's!

Rachel's dad wanted to take her out for ice cream after the concert, but she was afraid to ask her mother. Rachel was also too afraid to ask her mother for one of the extra three programs she noticed her mother saving, so she could give one to her father. Nancy knew what Rachel was thinking that time and whispered to her that her father gave an extra program to Rachel's father. Rachel was hoping that her mother would not be angry with Nancy's dad, but she was glad that her dad had a program. Rachel was even more relieved to have a friend like Nancy to help get her through the concert and understand how she felt after all.

Randall's Recital Rave- WOW!

Randall was playing the lead in his school play, written entirely by the students in his eighth grade drama class. They had rehearsed for two months solid, even on weekends. Randall was grateful that both is parents supported his interest in drama and were willing to drive him to and from the rehearsals at other cast member's homes. He had photocopied the schedule for both his parents since he lived one week at a time at each of their homes. The identical schedule was posted on the fridge at both his mother and his father's home. Randall was also thankful that his stepmother and stepfather came to his play, along with all his half bothers and sisters. His dad managed to save an entire row towards the front for both extended families! If Randall was embarrassed by having divorced parents, no one would have known by the look of pride he had on his face all night – his entire families on both sides were gathered to see him in his play tonight.

Randall never did as well on his report cards as any of his brothers or sisters or half brothers or sisters. Actually, he struggled to pass the grade each year with a reading disability, despite years of reading tutors and summer reading programs. Randall didn't need to read his lines, he memorized them almost immediately! When he discovered his interest in theater, his both parents agreed to sign him up for theater class after school. He had even applied for admission to a special high school for theater in the next community. This would involve both his parents transporting him there and back but both said they would if he really wanted to go and was accepted. Randall hoped more than anything to be accepted to Townsend Theater High School where he knew he would love to go to school each and every day.

There was a buzz in the boy's dressing room over by the door where the programs were just delivered. Parents had surprised their children by buying ads in the program to help support the theater club and congratulate their children. Randall did not expect an ad for himself since he forgot to bring home the advertisement request. Somehow, his parents must have found out about it, there was a giant half page ad with the name of every member of both his mother and father's family congratulating him!! There were also smaller congratulations ads from his grandmother on his dad's side, his aunt on his mom's side and even one from his dog, Socrates! Another advertisement in the business section for his step dad's business made five advertisements altogether, the most for any student in the play, a fact which his drama coach whispered to him.

This might actually be the best day of his life, Randall thought. When the play was over, he received more applause than any other thirteen year old straight A student ever received at an awards ceremony! His entire family was the loudest, of course. At the cast party in the school cafeteria, everyone was giving Randall high fives, and even asking for his autograph. One of the prettiest girls in the school said she was sure he would become famous and wanted him to remember her!! Randall brought his drama coach over to meet his family, all of them, and introduced him to each of his brothers and sisters, never mentioning half or step. Randall's coach had already met all four of his parents at the rehearsals and fundraisers over the past months. It was the drama coach who told his parents about the special high school, and tonight Randall heard him telling his parents that there was a scout in the audience from Townsend Theater High School who asked him specifically about Randall!

Pictures were being taken in every combination of family members with Randall. He thought he would go blind from all the flashes! Blind or seeing, Randall wanted the day to go on forever. When it was time to go home, he found himself unable to take the smile off of his face. At least, no one teased him for gloating! It was only Friday evening and he had two more performances to go, one on Saturday and one on Sunday. Randall didn't expect his family to show up again, but his mom and step dad were there on Saturday, and his dad and step mom were there on Sunday. Each set of parents took him out for a special dinner after his play, and each even allowed him to invite a different friend each night. Randall couldn't wait to go back to school Monday. Maybe next week he would hear from Townsend Theater High School......

Rachel and Randall both had very loving parents who wanted the best for them. Rachel's mother was so overcome by bitterness towards her ex that it prevented her from considering how important Rachel's concert was to her. She attempted to use Rachel's concert as a courtroom, taking the opportunity to prove to Rachel, herself, her ex and the world that her ex was a bad person, a bad father and deserved to be recognized and punished for his actions. Randall's parents certainly had some negative feelings towards each other and the divorce, but no one would ever know it. They made an unspoken pact to utilize Randall's unique talent to make him feel special, important and hopeful for his future. They knew how badly he needed that, in light of his academic struggles and stress of alternating weeks living with two families.

Important points to remember about our child's school performances and games:

Rachel and Randall both had divorced families who loved them very much. Rachel's parents could not get beyond their own feelings to put her needs first. This is common with divorced parents and they would have likely behaved differently had someone explained to them how it felt from a teenage girl's perspective. You have an opportunity to think and behave more like Randall's divorced families who recognized the unique opportunity to make him feel special and competent. This is especially important for children with divorced families, since they often spend much time trying to please both sides. Take the time to consider how you can make your child's recital, play, concert or game a special time for them to help ensure a healthy self esteem. Nothing beats seeing that look of pride on your child's face and you will feel proud as a parent as well.

Chapter Thirty

Volunteering: Vipers or Visions

*Why do schools need volunteers?
Schools wish to do the best job possible of educating their children and this task requires many more hours of work than available money and paid staff.

*How can I learn of the volunteer opportunities at our child's school?
Volunteer opportunities at your child's school will be posted in the newsletter and announced at PTA meetings. Flyers are sent home letting families know of the need for volunteers for different areas of the school functioning.

*What if do not have any time to volunteer at our child's school?
Volunteering may be required at certain charter or private schools; however it is voluntary at public schools. There will be no disadvantage to your child if you do not choose to volunteer.

*Are there special skills or services I can volunteer for our child's school?
Volunteers are needed in all areas of the school including office/clerical, cafeteria, bus and carpool lines, art, music, media center, computers, classroom helper, and more.

*What are the benefits of volunteering at our child's school?
You will have a first hand opportunity to see how the school operates, get to know the staff and understand the experiences your child has by volunteering at school.

*How will my volunteering affect our child?
Your child may feel proud of your contribution and become more motivated to be successful at school if you are volunteering there.

Do volunteers need to be fingerprinted and screened?

Many large school districts are requiring complete police background screenings and fingerprinting for the safety of the students. Check with your child's school district for the requirements.

Can my partner or my child's grandparent volunteer at school?

Schools often accept volunteers from the community who wish to be of service as well as any family member available to donate their time.

Can I volunteer in our child's classroom?

Volunteering in your child's classroom may or may not be in your child's best interests. Check with your child's school for their policy and talk with your child's teacher regarding this. The policy varies from school to school and teacher to teacher.

What is our child's responsibility regarding parent volunteers?

Your child is responsible to treat all volunteers including parents with respect, courtesy and appreciation. Your child is responsible to bring home to both joint custody parents any notices requesting volunteers at school.

How can we make our volunteering a positive experience for our child?

Discuss with your child your plans to volunteer at their school ahead of time and conduct yourself responsibly while there. Do not use volunteering as an opportunity to request additional consideration, special treatment or privileges for your child. Enjoy your experience of sharing your skills with an organization that benefits your child!

"Vance's Volunteering Viper – Oops!"

Vance's mother agreed to volunteer at his school for the book fair. She would work the cash register two nights in a row, since she worked days she did not need to take time off work. Vance knew his mother would do a great job since she had a job as a cashier at a large bookstore in their town. He was so proud to tell the PTA president that his mom would be the best person for the job; he couldn't wait to ask his mom. Thankfully, she said yes, although Vance was a little worried that she might not. Since his parents divorce, his mom seemed sad all the time. He was only nine years old but knew it was different from how his mom acted when she was married and happy. Since the divorce six months ago, Vance's mom was often too tired to do things with Vance in the evenings and on weekends. He loved his mother, but looked forward to going to see his dad every other weekend and Wednesday evenings because his dad was always full of energy. They played ball, rode bicycles, ran around the park and just kept going until Vance was exhausted and fell asleep watching TV. Vance's mom fell asleep watching TV each night and Vance had to wake her up to remind her to go to bed. He wondered why she was so tired and worried that being sad was making his mom tired. Maybe volunteering at his school book fair would make her happy. As promised, Vance's dad came to the book fair on the second day and bought him a book. Vance got to pick out any book he wanted and he selected a book about volcanoes, tornados and blizzards. His dad and he planned to begin to read it that weekend and every night he slept at his dad's until it was finished. They agreed to then borrow a library book about weather, Vance's favorite subject, after Vance got his first public library card. He couldn't wait! Just when he was smiling his broadest smile as his mom was ringing up his new book and his dad was paying for it, he was shocked to hear his parents raise their voices to each other. Vance didn't understand the entire argument but he knew it was about money. His father left angrily, almost forgetting to say goodbye to Vance. His mother was being consoled by the other volunteer cashier. Vance thought he heard her say to his mother something bad about all men. Were his mother and the other cashier thinking that all men were bad? Wasn't Vance going to grow up to be a man? Did that mean that he would be bad? Was his father really a bad man like his mother and the other cashier were saying? Suddenly Vance wanted to go home. He was sorry that he even asked his mom to volunteer. He didn't even care about his new book about the weather and was hoping that none of the children in his class knew what happened. Vance wished his mother would never volunteer again. He wasn't even sure if he still liked books or even wanted a library card.

"Valerie's Volunteering Vision – WOW!"

Valerie's mother agreed to be the volunteer in her daughter's fifth grade class to make telephone calls to the student's parents as important school events occurred during the year to remind them to attend. Some families were so busy that they misplaced flyers sent home or their children forgot to bring the notices home. Valerie's teacher found that a personal telephone call from another parent was a welcome reminder and had permission from the parents to give Valerie's mom their phone number. It was the third time this school year she was to make her calls, a task Valerie's mother really enjoyed. Since Valerie's parents divorce, Valerie noticed that her mom enjoyed talking to other parents about raising their children. Valerie didn't mind, it actually helped her make new friends as her mother made friends with her classmates' mothers. Tonight, Valerie's mom was phoning parents to let them know of the winter concert at school, and Valerie's class would be singing. Valerie knew how much her mother loved the phoning even though she worked all day as a customer service representative on the telephone. That night, however, Valerie noticed that her mother was feeling ill. She worried about her mother, but was also worried about the telephone calls. Valerie decided to call her father and ask him what to do. He asked Valerie to give the phone to her mother, but she was worried that her mother might not like that she called her dad for help. Valerie's mom always liked to solve her own problems and often told Valerie it was not necessary to call her dad every time something went wrong in the house. She was right and Valerie delighted in seeing her mother learn to fix things like her dad used to. But tonight was different, her mom was sick and Valerie didn't think that could be fixed in one night. When her mom hung up after talking to her dad, she explained to Valerie that it was fine that she called her dad for help. Valerie's dad was coming over to pick up all the phone numbers and make the phone calls for her mom! And, he was bringing some medicine for her mom as well. Valerie's mom explained that it was just a stomach virus and nothing to worry about. Valerie was glad that her mother would be okay and was also glad that her father would take care of the phone calls. Valerie thought about how her parents had kept their promise to work together to help her in school since their divorce two years ago. She knew if her dad was making the volunteer phone calls for her mom and bringing her medicine that they really meant what they said. It made Valerie feel safe and secure about her future, even if her parents were divorced.

Important points to remember about volunteering at your child's school

Maintain confidentiality with any information you learn about students, teachers and staff while volunteering at your child's school. It is especially important not to discuss with your child any personal information you may learn about their teacher or class-mates.

Parent Teacher Association Meetings: Madhouses or Missions

What is the role of the Parent Teacher Association?
What are the other parent groups at our child's school?

The Parent Teacher Association (PTA) organizes to provide support to the functioning of your child's school and provides input into school policies. Some other parent organizations are Parent Teacher Organization (PTO) and School Advisory Team (SIT). Inquire at your child's school to learn of the parent organizations at school.

How often do these groups meet?
How can I find out the schedule of meetings?

The PTA may have monthly meetings to discuss business and committee meetings to plan for events, fund raisers and special projects. Check with your child's school office for the schedule of the PTA meetings.

Is everyone invited – can I bring my partner? Can my ex bring their partner?

Everyone in the community who has an interest in providing support to your child's school is invited to attend.

Why do they elect officers?

Most PTA's are part of a statewide or national group which complies with an organized standard of meeting. In addition, funds are collected and there is a budget to manage.

Chapter Thirty-One: *Parent Teacher Association Meetings: Madhouses or Missions*

Can I attend just the ones I am able to or do I have to commit to attending all?

You are welcome to attend any one of the meetings and/or functions offered by the parent organization which interest you or are convenient. It is not necessary for you to attend all of the meetings unless you are an officer.

Do these groups really have influence over school policies and procedures?

While the amount of actual influence varies from district to district, many parent organizations have a great deal of influence over school policies and procedures.

Will the principal and other support staff be at these meetings?

The principal or a member of the support staff will generally be at the parent organization meetings. This is an opportunity for you to get to meet the people who manage your child's school.

Is this really important enough for me to get a babysitter in order to attend?

You may feel strongly about a particular issue at your child's school and this is the best format to discuss your concerns with other parents and pursue change. The PTA often sponsors activities which include families such as a book fair or ice cream party. Some schools arrange for babysitting or homework help during PTA meetings.

What is our child's responsibility regarding the PTA and other parent groups?

Your child is responsible to bring home notices to you announcing the meeting times.

How can my participation in the PTA benefit our child?

Your participation in the PTA may help influence policy at your child's school. You will also have an opportunity to meet school support staff and get a better understanding of the education process. Your attendance at PTA gives a message to your child that you care about their school.

"Millie's PTA Meeting Madhouse – Oops!"

Millie's mom was surprised to see her ex husband at their daughter's school PTA meeting since he had never been there before. And it surprised her further that he was on the agenda under new business. Her surprise turned to humiliation when he spoke of an idea that schools be required to send notices home to both joint custody parents, along with report cards, progress reports, newsletters and all communication from the school. How could he possibly think that this was the forum to complain about her lack of cooperation, Millie's mom wondered. She would have spoken but she had turned red and was frozen, she couldn't even move. Maybe she had forgotten to give Millie's dad copies of school information, but he did not need to publicly humiliate her in front of the PTA parents, teachers and principal of the school! Maybe if he remembered to pay his child support on time she would remember to provide him with copies of their daughter's school reports. Then maybe he would deserve to be a father to their beautiful, wonderful eight year old daughter, Millie. She wondered why the court could not see that he did not deserve to spend time with his daughter since he left the marriage. Leaving was his choice, not hers. Surely, Millie knew that since Millie's mom made sure to remind her frequently in case she ever forgot. Millie's mom couldn't understand why Millie adored her father so much after he divorced her mother. Wait until she hears about how her father came back into Millie's mother's life at the PTA meeting just to hurt her further. Millie's mother could not wait to get home and tell her daughter. Finally, Millie will see how horrible her father was!

"Max's PTA Meeting Mission – WOW!"

Max's teacher made a special announcement to the class of sixth grade students asking them to encourage their parents to attend the PTA meeting that evening. School safety was the topic of discussion and there was going to be a representative from the police department as well as local merchants and business owners. Incidences of violence in the community worried many parents and they asked to have improved safety measures at the Middle School. Some parents in the community felt that the measures being discussed such as metal detectors would make the school seem like a prison and scare their children. The topic was to be hotly debated after the police department presented statistics on violence and ideas to improve safety. Max knew this was important so he made sure to tell both his mother and father, even though they were divorced. They did have joint custody and explained to him at the time of the divorce two years ago that they both would remain involved with all important aspects of his life, including school. Max's parents also explained to him that it was his responsibility to let both of his parents know when there was an important school event. It took some time for Max to get used to telling both his parents. Before the divorce, he only told his mom and she told his dad. Now, it was his responsibility to tell his dad and his mom gently reminded him whenever he told her about a school event. She explained that it was her responsibility to make sure his father knew of school events, even though Max needed to be the one to tell him. Max didn't mind at all: he liked to call his dad and spoke with him almost every day over the phone. He only got to see him on weekends since his dad worked the late shift, but sometimes his dad took time off from work if it was really important. Max wondered if this was really an important meeting to be at, and his dad said that he would trade work shifts and go to the PTA meeting. He told Max that school safety was a concern of his and he wanted to be there to hear what would be presented. When Max's mother arrived, there were plenty of seats but they were filling up fast. She knew her ex husband would be late due to his work schedule so she saved a seat for him. He was only ten minutes late, but the auditorium was packed and there were no seats left so he was very thankful that his ex wife saved him a seat. Max's parents didn't really like to sit with each other too often, but no one would ever have known. They were at all of Max's recitals, sports games and other special events. One of Max's classmates asked him if his parents had remarried since he was surprised that they were nice to each other. Max knew that his friend's divorced parents fought in public and he felt sorry for his friend. The PTA meeting was very interesting and the parents were told they would be voting at a later meeting after more research was done. Max was glad that both his parents attended the PTA meeting as well as his other school events. He was glad that he remembered to call his father and that he had gotten into the habit of telling both parents about his school events. Max knew he was lucky to have parents that were nice to each other, even if they were divorced.

---

*Important points to remember about PTA Meetings

If your work schedule permits, make a point of attending at least one PTA meeting during the school year. Many important school management issues are discussed and you will be glad to hear the information first hand, give your opinion and influence policy. Your input will help make your child's school a better place!

Chapter Thirty-Two

Graduation: Gargoyles or Gaiety

What is the purpose of a graduation ceremony?
Graduation ceremonies are held to acknowledge and honor the hard work involved in a significant rite of passage for children. Families wish to share their joy and express their pride in seeing their children progress through school.

Which grades have graduation ceremonies?
Some school districts conduct only high school graduations, where others may hold elementary school, middle school and kindergarten graduations as well.

Where are the graduation ceremonies generally held?
Graduation ceremonies are held at your child's school if they have an auditorium large enough to seat all the graduates and their families. Alternative locations can be a community center, theater, stadium, or any facility large enough to seat all the graduates and their families.

How far in advance can I find out the date of the graduation ceremony?
Large facilities are generally booked well in advance. Most high schools will plan the graduation date at the beginning of the school year.

Who is invited to the graduation ceremony?
Family members and friends are encouraged to attend high school graduations. Some large school districts have limited seating and provide a limited number of tickets to each graduate.

173

*Should I bring my partner? Should my ex bring their partner?

If the partners of joint custody divorced parents have been involved in your child's educational career, it is appropriate for them to attend the graduation ceremonies.

*What about siblings, grandparents and other relatives?
*Is this important enough to invite out of town relatives?
*What if the school only allows a certain number of tickets to the ceremony?

If siblings, grandparents, other relatives and out of town guests are able to and wish to attend, your child will benefit from the additional pride in the audience for their graduation ceremony. Young children may find it difficult to sit still and enjoy the ceremony. If only a limited number of tickers are issued due to space in the facility, consider inviting guests to a dinner or party honoring your graduate.

*Can we take pictures? Who should be in the pictures?

You will want to take pictures of your child graduating and accepting their diploma. Memories of the occasion can be made with pictures of your child with all family members, including your ex.

*Do we need to sit together?

If you and your ex are not comfortable sitting next to each other, it would be in the best interest of your graduate if you were to sit in rows near each other. This is their important day, and you would be minimizing stress if your child did not have to alternate their gaze in different directions finding their two sets of parents in the audience.

*Which parent should pay for the cap and gown or other fees?

Discuss these fees with your ex ahead of time and come to an agreement. This is a happy time for your child and therefore would be unfortunate if their pride was blunted by a disagreement between their parents about paying these fees. If your child has a job, it might be appropriate to have them contribute to the fees.

*If we have a party for our child, do I have to invite my ex?

This is an important time in your child's life and they will probably wish to share their pride with both joint custody divorced parents. Excluding one parent from a party in your child's honor may be hurtful to your child.

Is this an important event for our child?

Graduation is a rite of passage which children hear about, read about and see in society throughout their lives. After working hard in school for years, it is likely that your child will find their own graduation to be a significant event in their lives.

What is our child's responsibility regarding their graduation ceremony?

Your child is responsible to take care of all the graduation requirements, and let both joint custody divorced parents know of the graduation date. Your child is responsible to behave appropriately during graduation ceremonies and show appreciation to their guests.

How can we make this a happy, memorable event for our child?

You can make this a happy memorable event for your child by demonstrating your pride in their accomplishments. Attending the graduation, inviting guests, taking pictures and having a family party will help make this a memorable event for your child.

"Gary's Graduation Gargoyle – Oops!"

Gary decided he would skip his graduation ceremony from high school. He would still get his diploma mailed to him and would still be considered a graduate but nothing was worth going through the same big mess he had to go through with his feuding divorced parents for every school function throughout his entire school career. He had turned eighteen just a few months earlier and had been thinking about this all school year. Gary felt entitled to make this decision and felt in his heart that it was best. He could not remember the number of counselors he met with over the years in order to help him adjust to his parents divorce. Each one would advise him to tell his parents how he felt and how their fighting affected him. At first Gary was afraid to tell them, but finally did with his counselor's help when he was thirteen. Later, Gary was angry that they didn't listen to his feelings; they just blamed each other and promised to try harder. Then there would be another awards assembly or music recital with an argument of who was to drive him or take him out after to celebrate or pay for his uniform. They both claimed to love him very much and want to spend time with him, but Gary's parents reminded him of children who could not share. Last year the discussion about the graduation ceremony started with his mother saying that his father was not allowed to take his new girlfriend to Gary's graduation ceremony. How could she even predict if the same woman would be in his father's life in a year? (It turned out she was not) Gary's father said that Gary's mother's sister could not come to the ceremony because she had insulted him and treated him disrespectfully in public at Gary's last music recital. This argument about who could and who could not come to Gary's graduation ceremony went on for an entire year until last night when Gary told both his parents simultaneously about his plan to skip the ceremony. He wrote a letter and made a copy for each one. Then Gary phoned them at exactly the same time (he borrowed a cell phone from a friend so he could do this) and told them each where in their respective homes they could find their letter. Gary wanted to make sure that each knew that they were being blamed equally by him for the fighting. The letter was a work of art. Gary wrote and rewrote about all his feelings over the years and why he had enough and would skip the graduation ceremony. Gary showed the letter to his school Guidance Counselor who was moved to tears. She had been one of the counselors in the long line who was unsuccessful in helping Gary's parents see the effect their fighting was having on Gary. She wanted to try to convince Gary to go to the ceremony anyway, but knew that his mind was made up and he would be able to move on finally. During the graduation ceremony when Gary's name was called, he was not there to go up on stage to get his diploma. His parents who loved him so much were not in the audience to witness this rite of passage and take pictures. Gary had decided to spend the day at the most relaxing place he had ever been to – the beach. He was at the beach for the entire day, feeling a tremendous sense of relief and looking forward to his first college semester in the summer, out of town, beginning in two weeks. Maybe by the time he graduated college, his parents will have stopped fighting and will both be at his college graduation ceremony. Or maybe he would no longer care if they were fighting once he began his life away from them. Gary wondered if they would still argue and what they would argue about with him gone.

"Glenda's Graduation Gaiety – WOW!"

After twelve years of school, not including kindergarten, Glenda could not believe that she was finally graduating!! Her parents and all the adults were right about doing homework and studying hard, although she didn't always think so at the time. Graduation felt like a reward for Glenda for her hard work. Glenda's grades slipped only one year in the middle of seventh grade when her parents surprised her with news of their getting a divorce. Glenda knew that she shouldn't have really been surprised since she had been aware that her parents were fighting and no longer good friends to each other. She even overheard a telephone conversation that her mother had with a friend where she told her about the plan for divorce. Glenda knew she should not have been eavesdropping so she pretended she never heard the conversation, just like she pretended that her parents were getting along just fine and would never get a divorce. When the truth came out, Glenda could no longer pretend, which was at least a relief from the stress of living with feuding parents and fear of divorce. After the divorce was finally settled, some things actually did get better and some things changed but were fine. Glenda lived with both parents for half the week, alternating the schedule as needed. She continued to remain close to both parents who took a consistent active interest in her schoolwork. Glenda still wished her parents never got a divorce, but she learned to accept it and got two additional bonus step parents and six step siblings throughout the years. Now, all four adults and six children were sitting in the audience waiting for her name to be announced to go on stage and accept her diploma. Glenda caught a glimpse of all ten of them in two rows on the left side of the auditorium, exactly where she told them to sit for the best view. Glenda was glad that her parents were no longer fighting and both seemed very happy. She could feel the pride emanating from her entire family and was glad that they would all be together for her celebration dinner. It was decided that she could pick her favorite restaurant and she picked the new barbeque restaurant in town which had the best barbeque sauce she ever had. Glenda was looking forward to her first dinner as a high school graduate with her entire family by her side.

> **Important points to remember about your child's school graduation*
>
> This event is for and about your child. There is no place for open hostility between divorced joint custody parents. In honor of your child, be exceedingly gracious to your ex during your child's graduation experience. Your child's memory of gracious parents will enhance their self esteem and sense of pride, something every graduate deserves!

Part IV

Negotiating an Agreement With Your Ex

Chapter Thirty-Three

Developing an Agreement

Where should we meet to discuss our agreement?

Joint custody divorced parents can meet anywhere to discuss their agreement regarding their children's' education, however, it would be best to meet in a neutral place such as a coffee shop. It is important that both parents feel that they are on equal ground; therefore a meeting at one of the parents' homes may not work out. As long as both feel free to discuss their thoughts and feelings at the location, it is not important what location is selected.

Should my current partner be included in this meeting? My ex's partner?

If your current partner and/or your ex's current partner plan to be part of your child's school career for the future, it would be appropriate to have them participate. If either parent feels uncomfortable with the current partner of their ex, it would be best to not include them.

What if I am single and my ex has a partner?

If you are single and your ex has a partner, it is fine for that partner to be included as long as the partner is involved in your child's education and you feel comfortable with that person.

Can grandparents and other relatives be included in the agreement?

If other family members are taking a major role in your child's education, it would be appropriate to include them in planning.

Should we consider our child's opinions in developing an agreement?

You should include your child's wishes in developing an agreement, however, keep in mind that children may not base their choices on what is in their best interests.

*Should our child be included in the meeting?

Some of the aspects of the discussion will center on money and other items that it might not be in your child's best interests to know the details of. Therefore, the best plan might be to include your child for part of the meeting and present the plan to your child as a united front once all the issues have been worked out by both joint custody parents. Make sure to remind your child of their responsibility regarding school.

*How long will this meeting take?

The length of the meeting will vary with different sets of joint custody parents. It might be necessary to end the meeting after a certain agreed upon amount of time and meet again to complete the rest of the agreement.

*What if my ex refuses to meet or discuss our child's schooling?
*What if my ex is not interested in taking part in our child's education?
*What if my ex fails to live up to their commitment?

It is unfortunate for your ex if they are not interested in their child's education. They will have lost out on an important part of their child's life. Joint custody provides both parents with the opportunity to participate in important aspects of their child's life; it does not legally require participation from both parents. It will be your responsibility to make sure your child knows how much you care about their education and it will become your sole responsibility to provide support, despite your ex's lack of interest. Check with your school Guidance Counselor for mentoring programs which might provide additional assistance and encouragement to your child.

*What if my ex and I cannot agree on all issues?

It is normal for happily married couples to not agree on all issues, and expected for joint custody divorced parents to have different opinions. In the best interest of your child, it is important that you reach an agreed upon compromise, despite your difference of opinions.

*How often do we need to review this agreement?

After the first agreement, it may only be necessary for you to meet briefly each year before the beginning of the school year to discuss new issues regarding school that will be coming up in the new school year. If the original agreement did not work out, it may be necessary to meet more often to renegotiate plans for the best interest of your child's educational needs.

Does the agreement need to be written?
It would be a good idea to take notes on the agreed upon decisions for the purpose of reminding yourself what you agreed to, not for the purpose of proving your ex irresponsible if they do not live up to their side of the agreement.

Should we formalize the agreement with notarized signatures?
Is this agreement something that can be used against me in court proceedings?
Shouldn't I check with my lawyer before signing anything?
If you and your ex are involved in a custody dispute or might be in the future, it is best to consult your attorney regarding any formal written agreements. However, you know what is best for your child, and the legal goals should not prevent you from discussing with your child's other parent about how you will both manage your child's school issues for the best interest of your child. A reputable attorney will represent your interests competently while advising you to always consider the best interests of your children.

What school issues should the agreement include?
Review the chapters in this book and consider which ones will pertain to your child. This might vary between children and change as they progress throughout their school years.

Should the agreement include other issues besides school?
If you and your ex wish, you may include other aspects of your child's life with your agreement about how to manage school. School issues are very concrete and present a good place to begin to negotiate your differences and compromise on an agreement.

What if I am unable to live up to my part of the agreement?
What if my circumstances change such as new job schedule or illness?
Circumstances such as illness, job changes and lack of knowledge may make it difficult to live up to your part of the agreement. It is best

to be honest with your ex, explain the circumstances and ask them to provide more assistance. It will be important to recruit relatives and close friends to help out in order to support your child's educational career. This is very difficult to do completely alone. For example, do not hesitate to ask a grandparent to attend a recital as your representative if you are unable to. You might be surprised to learn that relatives and friends are happy to help you instill a sense of pride and success in your child regarding their education.

What is the school's responsibility?

The school is responsible to provide notification to parents with as much advance notice as possible regarding school functions, homework expectations and rules and regulations at school. On a more general level, it is the responsibility of educational institutions to recognize that a growing number of children have joint custody parents, and become more sensitive to the needs of these families by developing procedures and policies to help support these parents for the best interest of the children.

What if the school does not live up to their responsibility?

You are encouraged to meet with the administration of your child's school and let them know of the specific needs of parents and children in joint custody families. Suggestions presented in a respectful, well thought out manor may encourage the development of procedures to meet these needs. For example, you might wish to request that extra copies of notices be sent home with children who have joint custody parents.

What are the responsibilities of our child regarding this agreement?

Your child is responsible to listen to the agreement presented by both joint custody parents regarding their school issues, let their needs and wishes be known, discuss aspects of school with both parents and bring home notices about school activities to both parents. It is also your child's responsibility to obey all school rules, complete their class work and homework, and study for tests.

What if our child does not live up to his or her part of the agreement?

It is important that both joint custody parents discuss how they wish to manage the situation if their child does not try their best in school.

Parenting styles vary widely regarding school expectations, rewards and consequences. If both parents agree and follow through on a united and consistent response, there is a better opportunity to help your child improve.

Should we show this agreement to our child?

Depending upon the age and maturity of your child, it may be best to discuss the major issues agreed upon between both joint custody parents, rather than showing them a written document.

Should we show this agreement to our child's teacher?

It is helpful for your child's teacher to be aware of certain aspects of your agreement so the appropriate parent may be contacted if needed. It is not necessary, nor appropriate for your child's teacher to be aware of all aspects of the agreement. Therefore, it would not be a good idea to give your child's teacher a copy of the agreement.

Do we need a separate agreement for each child?

Each child has different needs and therefore there will be some differences in the agreements. Many of the aspects may be the same; however, it is important to address each child's needs separately.

What else can we do to ensure developing a workable agreement?

Be flexible, be reasonable and put your child's best interests before your anger, disappointment and frustrations toward your ex.

Important parts of a workable agreement

A workable agreement will address who is responsible for each specific school issue, detail what the responsibility is, when and how often, and a timeline for participation.

Pitfalls to avoid in your agreement

Avoid volunteering for responsibilities you will not be able to fulfill. For example, you may agree at the moment to drive your child to and from additional tutoring three afternoons each week without considering that your job schedule will conflict with this responsibility. Avoid being distorted in your considering the needs of your child by letting your anger toward your ex guide your decisions to participate in your child's education. Avoid trying to seek a fair and equal amount of responsibility between you and your ex regarding school responsibilities. It is not often possible to obtain an equal split of responsibilities, nor is it necessarily in the best interest of your child. An equitable sharing makes the most sense – that is, each parent participates to the extent that they are reasonably able to. If each parent strives to participate one hundred percent, your child will receive the best possible support for their education.

Chapter Thirty-Four

Final Notes

Should we use a mediator, counselor or coach to help us develop an agreement?

If you and your child's other parent are not able to discuss school issues regarding your children without arguing and are therefore unable to come to an agreement on your own, it would be very helpful to hire a third neutral professional to assist. Ask your child's doctor, your attorney, or the local mental health association for a recommendation. Some states have begun assigning a Parent Coordinator through the courts to help divorced joint custody parents work out issues.

Are there other school support staff who are available to help us?

Your child's school Guidance Counselor can help you and your ex understand the normal developmental issues of children at various ages. Specific emotional and educational needs of your child and suggestions can be provided to both joint custody parents. Your child's school Guidance Counselor is neutral and will not be in a position to take sides with one parent over another, or mediate a dispute between divorced joint custody parents. The same holds true for the school Principal and other support staff.

What if I am still struggling to get past my anger and bitterness to-ward my ex?

It is normal to harbor resentment, anger and bitterness after a divorce. If you are aware that you are having trouble getting past it, then you are moving in the right direction. Consider consulting with a licensed therapist to address your feelings and learn coping skills to become happier and more successful in your life as an individual and as a parent. Your medical insurance company or your physician can refer you to an appropriate therapist. You can also contact the Mental Health Association in your community for a referral to both private therapists and public agencies.

What if my ex is confrontational or abusive to me?

It is not recommended to try to have a discussion with your ex or anyone who is confrontational or abusive to you. Any verbal threats or physical abuse should be reported to the police. This is in the best interest of your children as well as yourself.

What if my ex lives out of state?

If your ex lives out of state and is interested in being part of your child's education, there will need to be very creative planning with specific plans well in advance in order to participate in school events. Telephone and email contact with your child can be a great support to encourage motivation and even specific homework assistance.

Is there anything else I can do to increase the success of this agreement?

The success of the agreement will depend largely on the continuous positive communication between both joint custody parents. Make a concerted effort to contact your child's other parent regularly to inform them of school events and encourage your child to do the same. Avoid blame and fault finding when the agreement doesn't work out and plan on focusing how to improve plans instead.

How can I be sure that I am considering our child's needs first?

Consult with professionals who are aware of the educational, emotional, social and physical needs of children such as physicians and licensed therapists. Consult with professionals who are aware of your child's specific needs such as your child's teacher and school Guidance Counselor. You may find it difficult to sort through different opinions. It is normal for parents to continually question if they are making the best decisions for their children. Observe the outcomes and your child's responses to the decisions you have made in order to help you to put your best effort forth in continuing to make difficult parenting decisions.

How will I know if I need to attend parenting classes?
Can my ex be required to attend parenting classes as well?
* Should my partner and my ex's partner attend parenting classes?*

Most states require that divorcing couples who have children attend at least one parenting class in order to understand the feelings and needs of children during and after the divorce. There may be other parenting classes offered in your community which are a benefit for all parents to attend. If your partner and/or ex's partner participates in the parenting of your children, they can benefit from the classes as well. Specific topics such as discipline and homework scheduling are often addressed by speakers brought into your child's school through the PTA or Guidance Counselor. Check with your child's school for community referrals for parenting classes, as well as your child's physician or the mental health association in your community.

How will I know if I need to see a therapist for myself?
How will I know if our child needs counseling?

A licensed therapist can help parents and children sort through both normal developmental issues as well as those issues which fall outside the normal experience. Counseling and therapy today is not the same as the old stereotypical long term focus on past experiences. A licensed Marriage and Family Therapist is trained to address present issues in a short term program which will remove barriers to success and happiness for you and your children. Contact the American Association of Marriage and Family Therapy for a licensed therapist in your community.

Chapter Thirty-Five

Summary and Conclusions

*What are the most important things for me to remember?

Parenting children is one of the most difficult and rewarding life tasks you can experience. Just when you find something that seems to work, your child moves into a new developmental phase and you must learn many new ways of responding to their needs. What works for one child may not work for another. You will find yourself continually being a detective searching for clues as to how to help your child become successful and happy in their life. The suggestions in this book regarding specific school issues are helpful to all parents, not just divorced joint custody parents. Research has consistently found that children from divorced families, however, have greater needs in order to develop a healthy self esteem and a successful adult life. The good news is that research has also consistently found that when divorced parents respond to their children's needs, the difference between measures of self esteem, success and happiness between children from divorced parents and married parents no longer exists. In other words, divorced parents must work more diligently than married parents in order to provide for the emotional and educational needs of their children. The suggestions in this book help you select specific ways to help your children develop a healthy self esteem and successful educational career, as well as a happy, fulfilling future.

Resources

American Association of Marriage and Family Therapy
www.aamft.org/Therapist Locator/index.asp
703 838-9808

Mental Health America
(Formerly known as National Mental Health Association)
www.mentalhealthamerica.net
800 273-TALK

American Psychological Association
www.Practiceorg.locator.apahelpcenter.org
800 964-2000

Council for Exceptional Children
www.cec.sped.org
703 620 3660
1110 North Glebe Road, Suite 300
Arlington, VA 22201

Parents Without Partners International, Inc.
www.ParentsWithoutPartners.org
561 391-8833
1650 South Dixie Highway Suite 510
Boca Raton, FL 33432

Index